Ishtar's Songs:
Iraqi Poetry Since the 1970s

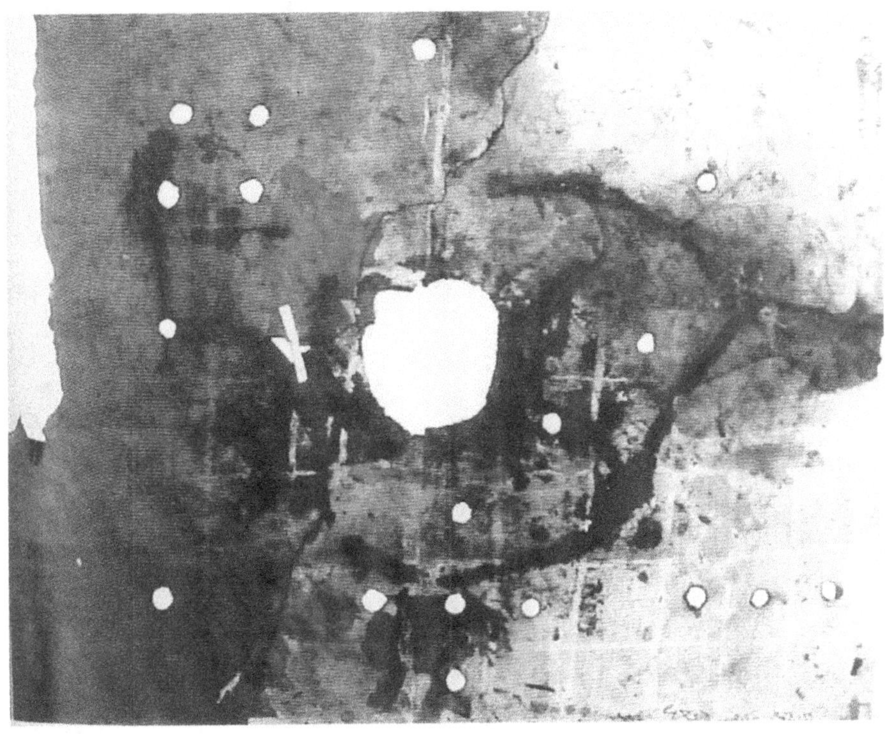

An Anthology

Edited by Soheil Najm

Translated by Soheil Najm and Dr. Sadek R. Mohammed
Poetry edited in English by Susan Bright

Plain View Press
P.O. 42255
Austin, TX 78704

plainviewpress.net
sb@plainviewpress.net
512-441-2452

ISBN: 978-1-935514-17-6
Library of Congress Number: 2010942081

Cover art: Sadiq Assaieg, sadiqart@hotmail.com
Title page art: Shakir H. Al Saeed
Cover design by Susan Bright

Sadiq Assaieg

Sadiq Assaieg: Born in Baghdad 1935.
Published book:
The Song of the Rhinoceros, Baghdad 1973

This Is Baghdad

For Tony Blair

This city is a miracle,
bombs thrown down at it,
smashed under our feet
like a broken watch,
yet,
as if reborn,
you can hear it ticking, under the debris,
you can sense its heart, and its lost parts.
A miracle city
in a state of dreaming and delirium;
history memorizes its poems.
Its houses are ruins
its buildings are forlorn,
yet colored flags
surrender to the touches of an April wind,
stable on the roofs, and masts
sewn with worn patches
designed with simple artistic sense
remain to hail the limits of agony and loss.

It throbs and gleams under the sun,
coloring the faces of the poor and the streets
with the colors of sky and angels.
It is a city afflicted with dreams of future.
Its body is in flame
and its faucet is dry.
There is wrath, hunger
and teeth gnashing in its depths.
A city that history,
snipers, lovers, poets,

invaders, barbarians and oil thieves are ravenous for.
In every age they thought it dead —
a very long cry erupts
from the depths of her soul,
circulates in her air like broken waves:
"To die or not to die,
to live or not to live
to be or not to be
that is the question".

Yesterday
pupils of the preliminary school,
who had survived one hell of a bombing,
went out of their classes to the alley,
played a long penalty kick
that split space like a flying dish,
sailing over laundry lines hung with wet clothes
to land, a new disaster,
breaking the neighbors' window.

At Abu-Ibrahim's café
which is well-known as the café of the "complicated group"
full of book lovers, poets and unemployed people,
human windpipes come to blows in a resounding debate,
this time about a prose poem.
It's the author, who is ready to fight anyone,
insists that it is designed according to "Dadaism".
That is why it is afflicted with the bird-flu virus,
"No need to say that it bears a
Suq Mureidy[1] signature,"
commented another man,
bestowed with mistrust for modern art,
after he set down a domino piece,
while some others argued about
a new play described as "popular,"
which someone described as the "essence
of misunderstanding"
of "pop" theory and visual art
after the World War, and

an acute wave of debate
blew up from the back row
about contents of the forth dimension,
Ibrahim al-Jaffari,[2]
Fokoyama,
and the end of history.

Not far from the hotel
of hajj Hamoodi al-Doori,
that is well-known as "The Greats' House"
at a public market
cars passed through crossing the bridge;
I saw them, in my eyes, flying,
speeding along the asphalt of the street
as if they were meteors,
a bride inside one of them,
she will lose her virginity this night—
the captain hajj Rzuqi
and the applause of a crowd of people
in the shop of hajj Hamodi al-Doori,
near al-Mutanabi Street,
a radio with a bad teeth sang
a song of sympathy for Zuhur Hussein[3]
then came a news broadcaster
to apologize about a mistake in broadcasting
and about a simple change
for the time of the news,
according to Greenwich time,
and at three o'clock
exactly as the last raid was over
an Indian parrot sang in Arabic —
before a crowd of children surrounding it —
a Kahttan al-Madfaie's[4] song "Mohammed O Mohammed."
Then it climbed in arrogance onto
an artificial green bough
delighted by its own long,
bow tail.

Amazing city as I said.
Snipers, prophets and killers are searching for it,
angels, poets and saints.
East and west.
North and south.
One of the most beautiful cities in the world,
its depths are rocked by bombing everyday
without losing is balance.
Although its women
are whispering to their men in low voices at night,
lest the children wake
yet the men don't hear despair,
they go on.

A miracle city
its crescents are always drunk,
and their stars are drunk too.
Although bombs are thrown down at it
and it is smashed like a broken watch,
yet it stays ticking.
As if it were reborn,
risen from garbage,
on broken light wings —
a code for the forthcoming generations,
its heart still throbbing and throbbing
like the singing nightingale alarm of the broadcast
ringing with all its strength, with power and steadiness,
in spite of everything remain
the words
this is Baghdad,
this is Baghdad,
this is Baghdad.

[1] Suq Mureidy: A public market in Baghdad.
[2] Ibrahim al-Jaffari: The Iraqi ex-prime minister.
[3] Zuhur Hussein: Iraqi woman singer who was well-known during the sixties.
[4] Kahttan al-Madfaie: Iraqi singer.

Translated by Soheil Najm

Acknowledgements

For their bright notes here and there on the translations I'd like to express my thanks to the New Zealand poet Mark Pirie and the American poet Susan Bright who contributed a final poetry edit of the text in English. Also special thanks to Dr. Mohammed Darweesh for his precious notes concerning the whole manuscript. Thanks to American poets, Mike Maggio and David Radavich for proof eading the final galleys.

Soheil Najm

Art by: Faysel Laibi.

Contents

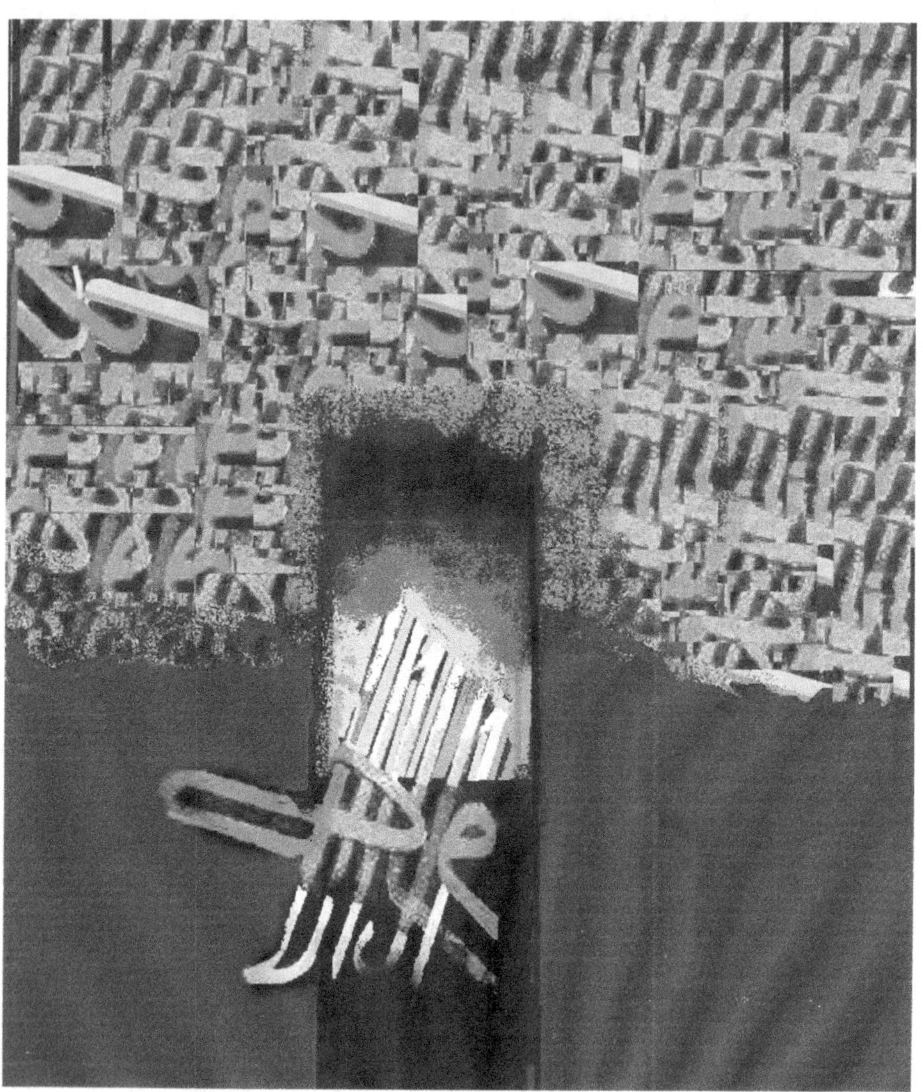

Art by Sadiq Assaieg.

Iraq: Poetry and Rebellion

If it is true that Iraqi people are rebellious and have a volatile disposition, we should see that mindset in Iraqi poetry, and so we do, from ancient Mesopotamia to the present day. Iraqis have registered revolt in poetry throughout history by consistently inventing new forms and bold ideas beginning with the eternal epic *Gilgamesh*, which sets up literature's first theme: the aesthetically beautiful and universal human search through death for immortality.

Iraq, since the dawn of history, has been an incubator for creativity. The first poet known to history emerged here, the Priestess, Enheduanna (2285-2250 BC) who wrote her poetry on the walls of the temple where she presided. She was the first educated female who had the ability to express herself in writing — something that could not have occurred in the absence of a cultural environment encouraging creativity. Her work is the very essence of revolt. The daughter of King Sargon of Agade, she wrote poetry critical of his wars: "You have filled the rivers with blood, and the people have nothing to drink."

In the Abbasid era of Islam (750 -1258), Iraq became a breeding ground for Arab poetry. Poets obsessed with creativity and rebellion arrived here. They made a new mark on poetry by breaking with their predecessors and creating new forms that were not confined by the screaming and indignation of reactionary poetry which forced poetry into forms that were impossible to reckon with life. Abu Nuwas (756-814), Abu Tammam (788 -845) and their generation began this revolt from traditional forms. The genius al-Mutanabi (915-965) took their innovations to a higher level.

The poets of Assyyab's generation (1926-1964), called the Generation of Pioneers, were greatly influenced by modernism in Europe which opened broad prospects for poetic expression and inspired the spirit of revolt integral to the Iraqi aesthetic. They turned their attention not only to the orchestral rhythm of Arabic poetry and the variegated harmonic but also to the work of finding a completely new poetic form rooted in the heart of the Arabic language itself. The achievement of Assyyab's generation was not just a rhythmic achievement, but also an intellectual one which widened the imagination of the poet and played us a symphony of intersecting voices, integrating the present with a system of imagination centuries old.

Dostoevsky warned us against killing the father, but the matter is not so simple to the poet driven by creative force. In the sixties a new generation of poets veered away from the Pioneers. They believed innovation to be deeply rooted in the psychology of every real poet and became fascinated with and researched new forms of poetry to speak ever more private realities and to make their art unique. The generation of the sixties did not rely upon direct expression, strict rhymes, or the romanticism or clarity of their predecessors. They were inclined to accept ambiguity, expressed alienation and embraced indirect expression crafted through images and connotations. They had to work hard to achieve credibility, with the guns of the fathers' criticism always poised to silence them.

The work of the poets of the sixties and their new styles were not settled in Iraqi literature for a long time, although its poets were (and some still are) continuing to give their poems to a literary milieu that was a mixture of the voices of the Pioneers and new voices. In the 1970s there were again ambitious attempts to change poetics, to engage everyday life in poetry. Some tried to force language into "pure poetry" forms, finding random relationships between words or images, emptying language of significance. You must remember this was a period of harsh political and social turmoil in Iraq.

Meanwhile, one new form was forbidden. Prose poems were not allowed to appear on the pages of cultural or literary magazines for two reasons, in my view. In the first place, the prose poem let the poet be spontaneous enough to pass over taboos surrounding politics, sex and religion. The second reason is that the government claimed to be the guardian of tradition, and this pattern of poetry was completely different from anything they had ever seen. Notice that the Iraqi government had a monopoly on publishing and printing and was able to curb freedom of expression and to fabricate complaints against "false, unrealistic and non-artistic poetry," adding to the authoritarian political system another black mark of repression.

The Iraqi poetic spirit of revolt did not yield during the 1980s to that authoritarian monopoly in publishing and printing. It carried the genes of overcoming in its blood. Surely there is a spiritual need to write new poetry that is an essential characteristic of poets. The Iraqi society of this era endured two wars. They were the most atrocious wars identified by Iraqi history. A catastrophic, nightmarish atmosphere dominated the joints of life and poets could not even sing lyrical poems or complain about waves of time and frustration—themes that dominated the Arab poetry of previous periods. Reality was so shocking to express it well the poets of the new genre, the prose poem, had to find new artistic styles for the Arabic poem — narritive fragmentation, dramatic structure, polyphony, the mixture of senses and emotional density in poetry that weren't know here before.

In the same way, the generation of Assyyab found awareness and understanding of contemporary life in the new world after World War II, and in the widespread global cultures they came to know. This stimulated a need to cross and then demolish old, established forms of poetry. Relying on the talents of the poet, they broke away from the monotony of classical music and forms. The new state of the war between Iraq and Iran created here, beginning the early 1980s, a storm of renewal in poetry. As a matter of fact, it was preceded by experiences inside and outside Iraq, but for the first time the poem took form in totally new directions. Poets created relationships and rhythms that were unfamiliar to the "taste" of Arabic poetry. Here was a final divorce from the traditional rhymes of Khalil ibn Ahmad Al Farahidi (the Arabic philologist c. 718–c. 791), the creation of new elements, an open horizon, a poetry completely free of familiar frameworks of metaphor and rhetoric.

I believe most Iraqi poets who came to poetry from the 1970s until now drove themselves to melt in the crucible of the creative experience that I have related above. But since the 1980s or perhaps shortly thereafter, the poet has also become aware, more than ever, of the danger of linguistic relationships full of explosive meanings. Thus poets were forced to batten down language at the same time new forms of their own invention were exploding. Poetry became images generated from crystal vision that inspired meaning without declaring its secrets. The play became more dangerous as the poet grasped the absolute freedom to structure his or her own imagination and was responsible for the consequences it wrought.

I would like to point out here, somewhat paradoxically and because art is indomitable, that the relationship between poetry and ideology had also loosened. Even though Iraq had experienced two wars and political oppression, the period of the eighties was a crucial period because many poets left ideology and allowed themselves all sorts of freedom in terms of both form and content. In spite of political restraints, the time of ideological domination that brutalized poetry and humiliated it to the flatness of political pedagogy had passed. A new poetics of revelation which feeds depths of the human soul and leads us to aesthetical contemplation of the universe and our place therein emerged.

The reader will find here rattling sounds of war, pain, tanks, appeals, complaints, as well as inner voices that complain of isolation and loneliness and wrestle the monster of distressing alienation. The Iraqi diaspora has caused a huge number of us to drift away to every corner of the world, and we hear those voices. Some poets call for Eros or love and sing in the pursuit of beauty. Some poets delve into deep and mystical questions about existence, calling out death and searching for a kind of certainty can pull worry from the soul.

Soheil Najm
Baghdad
Sept. 2010

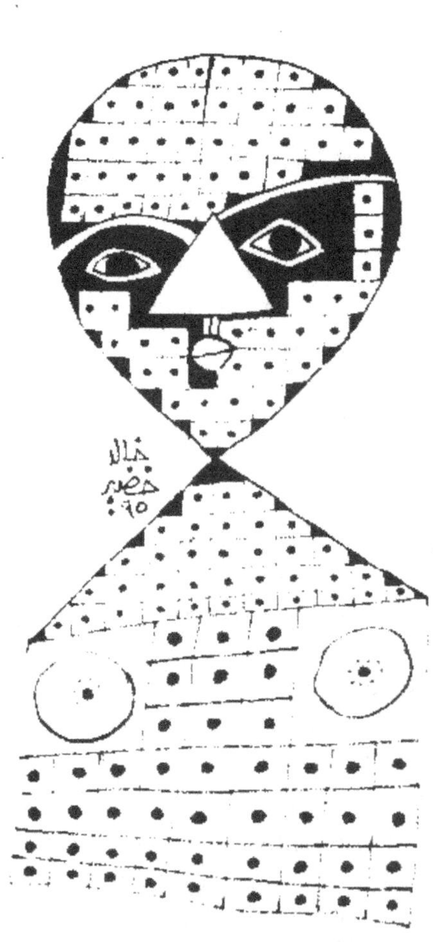

Art by Khalid Khudayer

Abbas al-Ali

Born in Baghdad, 1965.
Ph. D. in Arabic.

For Memory and Its Closets

Wearing Yousif's shirt
and Charlie Chaplin's trousers
trains look at me doubtfully,
bags sit in first class chairs,
bags that wear silver ties.

And I am hammering the pegs of my alienation
in the fever of the last-seat window.

When I stare at our old city walls
the train becomes a Cossack horse
playing the contrabass.
There is a moon not burnt yet
which was lit for the first time
the instant my mother's sight stumbled
in front of the needle of the sewing machine.
O mother, as vast as are our sins,
why do corpses alone
wear silk
in our naked countries?

Translated by: Soheil Najm

Abdussadah al – Basri
Born in Basra, 1967.

The Moon Courts It Every Night

Its mud rooms of whispers
never leave your life.
Rest there fills your lungs, a new fragrance.
From its windows sparrows go on pilgrimage,
play music…
dance…
and sing…
then use its cheek for a pillow
and sleep.
Through its doors, there are many visitors.
From its Christ's thorn there is a rustle.
The moon courts it every night
and the sun kisses its eyes every morning.
It still dwells in you
and travels with you —
the threshold,
your father's voice and your mother's lullaby,
the tobacco packet,
his stick and your little brother's entreats,
your dolls
the seesaws,
the date palms and the brook's murmur,
your brother's noise,
lost rubbers,
pencils tips,
your torn school books,
your bag that was full of wishes,
the days,
the ages you have lived and the age you are living,
the streams and the palm leaves,
the nightingale's singing,
their scattered nests,
the water *susurrus* every evening,
mud drops,

the Bamber glue[1],
your kite and the boats of your dreams,
grandmother's tales
and winter stove,
the relief of earth after rain,
your cradle bequeathed to your brothers,
your father's cough,
your mother, friend of weeping,
the cold,
the mud
by the wet cottage,
the alienation that is still dragging your feet,
it…
it…
it…
it lives in you always
that which is not as it was anymore!!!

Basra, 2002

[1] Bamber glue: A glue oozes from the Bamber tree which is known in Basrah.

Translated by: Soheil Najm

Abdul Settar Jabr Al-Asadi

Born in Baghdad, 1968.
Published book: *The Sparrow of Silence*, Baghdad, 2000.

The Dead Sea

We were barefoot,
the sea was running after us
the raindrops were chasing us…
We were gnawing dreams like dry bread,
and from among the sleeping trees
the moonlight
was washing our shabby clothes…
How, then, did the sparrows of the village fly?
Their excrement is still on the glass of our windows.
Did they beat the drums of freedom
O my country…?

O

Fear smiles shyly
within the soul
and lame memories wear out
hanging their stupidity on the clothes-line of the ports
and return without sails,
burying their sparrows in pockets full of holes
near the miserable streets over there,
kicking their loitering pebbles with the ecstasy of pain
to wait for hoarse voices as they push the wagon of silence
towards the void-ridden abyss…
and between the tide and the knife there is a line of the sea
puffing out air in the face of murdered fish.

○

There, we were watching, like children,
defeated colors in front of a paralyzed picture of a lake.
Our eyes preceded us in sipping oysters from wailing seagulls.
We were burying the sea in the sands.
We were making way for plague-infected ships to enter the city.
The distant darkness approaches like a stupid hour
carried by the wings of bats
that spread the wind everywhere
and peck the body of water
so the flesh of the sea is ripped apart
and seagulls escape behind the setting sun.
But we were still gazing fearfully
until bats stuck their picks in our eyes.
Since then we began another life:
seven blind men roaming cities,
singing for
The Dead Sea,
a slaughtered sun behind bars,
seagulls that drain the blood of the sea,
the lost distances in us,
and broken ships on the rocks of darkness…

Translated by: Dr. Sadek R. Mohammed

Boredom Window

The sun is colorless
and the earth has sold its dust
searching for pavement to sleep on.
I shall bury the dead where birds nest
and all night scrape scales from sea fish.
Maybe seagulls will travel to the shores.
I shall paint a picture of homeless cats
and write the civilization of homeless dogs
where whores curse God,
violently chew their naked bodies
then spit them out like empty chewing gum.
I shall devour daybreak
and chase sparrows standing on electric wires,
then return to my house to carve on the wall:
a window for the boredom crammed inside me.
The streets in my city are homeless
and the sleeping trees are dreaming of freedom.
I shall sail without a ship;
because I have nothing but one shirt
and a voiceless song.
I shall expel gypsies
and tear the papers of loafing time.
Ink is still trickling from my poetry collection hung
on a publication rope and my scorched body
is still emitting its dark ash on distant forests
and on shores that are jammed with dead seagulls.
O violet color: do you feel lonely?
Do you know how many silences are looking
for a distant corner?
Seaweed hates the color green
but loves the sea...

Translated by: Dr. Sadek R. Mohammed

Abdul-Khaliq Keitan
Born in Misan, Amara, 1969.
Published books: *The Displaced*, Beirut 1998,
Tramps of Baghdad, Amman and Beirut, 2000,
Waiting for the Marion, Beirut, 2000.

Or ...He Staggers Like a Dethroned King

For whom are all these joys which
heap up in the streets?
For whom...?
Buses make off with our youth and we say:
Once again the prices of cigarettes have gone up.
For whom, if not for the paupers, for instance?
The singers eat rice and drink chicken soup.
All right, this is a starless hotel
and yet
it shines with my prince friend and me...
joys, what plots!
Travelers like these leave their luggage in stations.
The ladies are without eyes this time.
Beautiful cars are not a dream anymore.
Everything is leaving or staggering like a dethroned king.
They are passionately fond of what?
And what safe havens are they looking for?
We need gigantic lockers to store our archives.
From Imarah[1] to Al-Rasheed street
there are no grocers.
Beloved women play the tragedy of their coughs
and youngsters poke fun at their teachers.
There are no grocers
and because he staggers,
we quietly look at disputes,
disputes that start from the bed
and do not end with the street.
The friendships that we make with beauty,
they too uncover our alleged brilliance
or let's say: "The holder of the two horns is not capable of
                tolerating all these trumpets.

He raised his two horns and knelt."
I shall praise the princesses
        "There is only one miracle.
          Man talks"
Granting all these crowds another chance,
is there an upcoming war?
Then we might look at joys with more justice…
move the singers away from the ring
and assume that statues would be urinals…
Where can I put all this pain?
I divided it among my friends and it still flows like blood.
I, now, shamelessly wave to the princesses
while they, with all humility, wave to the mirrors.
Corruption breeds nothing but insanity
causing streets to roar with random motion.
Quietly, O my statue
more quietly,
withdraw all these histories.
I shall upholster my memories and make a whistle out of them,
one whistle that can save this pregnant woman and then I say:
"How many other poems deserve this austerity on my part?
I am pining away, and my vehicle is getting old
no friendships from now on
because you do not even deserve that I see you!"

1994

[1]Imarah is a city in southern Iraq and is the birthplace of the poet.

Translated by: Dr. Sadek R. Mohammed

28

The Pain Sura

Every thing is tidy in the encampment of elegies:
the soldiers,
the flour,
misgivings,
only desire sleeps on white sheets
while soldiers rub flour with misgivings.
Why was my puberty delayed all this time?
Why have I grown old without going through adolescence?
Why the wrinkles, the photo albums and the archives?
Every thing,
the bereaved women,
the orphans,
the ones lost in war,
the ones with amputated legs.
Peace be upon my master and lord...peace be upon the protector
of bereaved women... the protector of orphans...
the protector of flour...peace be upon you for your patience...
Peace be upon your wounded brothers and their betrayed children
... for you sir,
for you, a country made of gold and ripened by bombs
until it became sand and wind!
So, we are stiffer than rural timber.
We smell fat and lick mirrors.
My pot bubbles with steam on its fire
while I have no pot or fire
and there is no steam.
I complain against you, O you who are of scant worth.
Should I sit quietly thinking every night, and the night never ends
and from one night to another, there is no morning,
as if the mornings were amassed in a winter chimney?
The fault is not mine.
Kitchens are sterile
and there is no miracle.
Peace be upon my father...peace be upon my mother...
upon my brothers...
Peace be upon men as they chew silence...
peace be upon women as they
cook teardrops...peace be upon brothers who have emigrated...

peace be upon the Euphrates, niggardly in its gifts to its people…
Everything advises everything.
No wars.
No leadership.
There is nothing but your resounding voice
banging mouths with ears
and drawing arches and hoses on our walls.
O what pain…
O you whom we spell in the secrecy of the temples!
We recite your signs in dry rooms.
We eulogize our isolation before you
and we embalm desires in front of you.
For you is all obedience and we are at your beck and call.
Peace be upon you
upon your shades as they protect foreheads,
peace be upon your silver in place of the gold of speech,
peace be upon your sealed records,
upon the signatures,
the poems,
the soldiers,
the flour,
the misgivings.
Peace be upon us as you squeeze us
and we have no option but to bow.

1995

Translated by: Dr. Sadek R. Mohammed

Abdul-Mutalib Mahmood
Born in Baghdad 1950.
Published books:
I Woke Up From Childhood…Don't You Ever Wake Up, Baghdad, 1980,
Perhaps I Was Amongthem, A Novel, Baghdad, 1982,
Before War…After War, Poems, Baghdad, 1983,
The Third Balcony, Poems, Baghdad, 1987,
Late Apology For Childhood, Damascus, 2000.

Possibilities

(from an old notebook)

Call me a forest…and reside in me
or a planet…and throw me outside the universe
or a stone…and leave me on the brink of the river
and smile…as you like to smile.
Start from just a doubt,
steps between us will get closer
and a night will entertain two lovers not like all other nights,
or start from your doubts,
you will find me…a forest,
a planet,
or a stone.
It is a moment between two extremes,
between two possibilities,
the nearest to you…is the farthest.
"The nearest to you prompts this madness!"
What's wrong with you? Why do you manifest the cruelty of a woman
never visited by sparrows…
never celebrated once the rain?

○

Like this you are…
You were a possibility that turned me over to doubts
and became a presence sharing with me the joy of the moment…
and ruined me.

Then you exaggerated good-hearted fear
and I was afflicted with a worry dazzling in its surprises…
and I called your love: madness!
32

July, 1979

My Dead Ones Are Waiting at the Door

My dead ones are waiting at the door. Shall I open?
I am hesitant…I fear the slipping away of the door.
I fear being touched by impossible hands
and follow the traces of steps that might mislead me.
I fear that faces might look upon me like twilight
and I become ashamed of them…
and can not find expressions to hide my misgivings.

☽

They are my dead ones…waiting at the door.
They have not become weary of standing,
but I have become tired.
They will forgive my hesitance,
and understand all my reasons,
and might leave me and go away,
and thus leave me between the dreams
of the beginning and eternity.

But they are my dead ones…
I discern in their features the lines of my palm.
I try to hide the boy they granted to
the world…but he lost himself in poetry,
in waves of captivating eyes,
and in the futile journey of time!

☽

My dead ones are waiting…
A crowd of faces,
some are radiant…and some are sullen and wrinkled.
Shall I open?
This door separates us and I am here…
hesitant, fearing the slipping away of the door,
creating engagements to deal out my worries among them
and looking for expressions befitting their love…

O

My dead ones… O my dead ones!
You are the secret love cord
between the beginning… and eternity.
You are a course of lives spent
in ages, their years are still passing,
rotating like orbits,
traversing, like fillies, the restive journey…
of the body-deriding spirit…

I am here, worried…
I can not find expressions to hide my misgivings…
Fatigued by poetry,
fatigued by concerns other than yours,
I have reasons to reside behind this door
and behind that door…many doors
and I have a wife and children…and a limitless horizon!

O

My dead ones move along together,
heading for the vast space.
They are crossing the impossible.
Their hands are in its hand,
and I am here with them.
They are around me…some trifle with my child
and laugh…
but I…
do not see any of them!

Translated by: Dr. Sadek R. Mohammed

Abdul-Zahra Zeki
Born in Baghdad, 1955.
Published books:
The Hand Discovers, Baghdad 1995,
The Book of Paradise, Baghdad 2000,
The Book of Today, the Book of the Magician, Ramallah, 2001.

The Wine of the Sultans

Where have you been sleeping?

Your night was a diamond
and your bed was the wine of the Sultans.
Your dreams were lifting your night
and guarding your bed.

The diamond was thawing on your two nipples
and wine was streaming on your navel.
Your sleep was an ethereal sea.
Its waves were your dreams crawling on your thighs
and under your feet, fire was passing the night
awake, blazing flames and smoke.

Translated by: Dr. Sadek R. Mohammed

The Bones of the Hoopoe

Leave him!
The gentleman who inflames the waves
with the bones of the hoopoe.
Leave him!
His hammer polishes the clouds
as if your hands were fires
very high
waving for him.

Translated by: Dr. Sadek R. Mohammed

Experiment

Yes,
we renounced gold because of the voice.
But there was no gold
and there was no voice.

We imagined gold
so as to imagine the voice.

Translated by: Dr. Sadek R. Mohammed

Abdul –Kareem Kasid

Born in Basra, 1947.
Published books:
The Bags, Beirut 1975.
Knocking on Childhood Doors, Baghdad, 1978.
The Gravestone, Beirut, 1981.
The Picnic of Pains, Sahara House, 1990.
Sarabad, Beirut, 1998.

The Ideal City

The city I crossed to
on a wind carpet,
a sand horse
and a paper boat,
the city that betrayed me
by ten candles
and a sly meow,
the city that conjured me as a salt pillar
is crossing me now
on a wind carpet,
a sand horse
and a paper boat.

Translated by: Dr. Sadek R. Mohammed

The Ephemeral

You are neither history
nor geography
in our maps,
which are attributed to another age,
where the sky is colored grey
and the earth has the size of a hoof
and the country looks like ant villages.

You are not history
nor geography,
O you, who are attributed to us
as moss is attributed to the sea
as an epidemic is attributed to God.

Translated by: Dr. Sadek R. Mohammed

Adeeb Kamal Ad-Deen

Born in Baghdad, 1953.
Published books:
Details, Baghdad, 1976,
Divan, Baghdad, 1981,
The News of the Meaning, Baghdad, 1996.

An Attempt at Madness

(1)

The moon is at the door
hanging by its feet.

(2)

Everyone became introverted
like a broken string.

(3)

Friends multiplied, here or there,
as lies and nonsense.

(4)

The meaning is detained in itself,
no one can ransom it,
not even I.

(5)

Those who died
wrote their subverted poems.

(6)

Yesterday I died
and in the morning, as usual, I woke up.

(7)

Hunger is a letter.
All you need is to put it
in an envelope
and send to yourself.
Sorry,
To me.

(8)

The woman died: the dream, the meaning and the dawn died too.
Her death was an occasion for forty disasters.

(9)

Madness is beautiful
because it is my full-of-birds post office box
and my full-of-darkness future.

(10)

My letters protested
against the mountains of grief in them
so I repressed them with an iron fist
and patience and horror.

(11)

The poet and the ruler died,
the philosopher died,
and the historian died,
but when the grocer died
only then did the people protest.

(12)

The only friend who survived,
sent me a letter full of serpents and owls.
It filled my house with horror.

(13)

When I read my poems in a public
celebration yesterday,
there was a huge crowd of people
I'd never dreamt of.
There was only my heart,
my table,
and my blood.

(14)
Your love is a light sign
and you, my love, are
a prophetess of darkness.

(15)

When I wrote your name, I became confused.
I madly loved its letters.
I feared that people might behold them,
rather I feared that I would behold them myself.

(16)

Where are you
to bring back the drums of Africa,
the cock-and-bull stories of Asia
and the phantoms of the lower world to my blood?

(17)

Your love has become a poem
infatuating all the fools of the earth.
How wonderful!

(18)

Your love led my poetry
to the essence of letters and dots
and led me to superiority
nay, to superior madness!

(19)

Th..........
The moon is at the door.
It has lifted one of its feet!

Translated by: Dr. Sadek R. Mohammed

Adil Abdullah
Born in Baghdad 1955.
Published book:
The Museum of Nothingness, Baghdad.

Collective Unemployment

Everybody here is out of work,
the workers in the factories and the civil servants in offices
all of them are out of work!
Those who are going early to the farms
and coming back tired at noon
are also out of work.
The students and the teachers who the government
is keen to provide with plentiful gifts
to remain jobless are also out of work.
The army and the police,
the children and the adults,
the women in the houses,
the old men in the mosques all of them are
out of work!
When strangers blanket darkness
upon a country
there will be no work for its citizens
but to return sunrise to its extinguished sun.

Translated by: Soheil Najm

The Prey

Like a flock of eagles on a wounded prey
his fancies met here in Iraq,
in spite of all the hatred and the discord among them
they returned to their homes
through the darkness not caring for the blood
on their mouths.
But what vast shame will touch their souls in the morning
when they discover by its light
that what they ate yesterday
was the flesh of their sons.

Translated by: Soheil Najm

Adil Mardan

Born in Basra, 1956.
Published books:
Oriental Spaces, Madrid 1999,
One Who the Calmness Couldn't Attend Him, Basra, 2005.

Statues Watching Nothingness

The predatory birds hit the rock
and fly aloft.
Soft
and gloomy
surfaces—
Where are the pomegranate blossoms?
Where is the harvest?
The optimistic viewer
on a plastic bench
allocates a bouquet of artificial plants.
Perplexed statues on the benches
watch nothingness.

Now who can cross the Acacia
to the extreme statue
where the stone ancestors sleep?
Who is the moving statue now in front of the window
watching the pomegranate blossoms?
Go to sleep O boulder rock, surrounded by slander.
The peasant goes back to watering,
cuts some pebbles
to play with the statue of his eyes.
You too, my stone,
know why they call me the slave.

The peasant deals with indoor plants
and washes his hands with antiseptic.
The surfaces are soft and gloomy.
The predatory birds fly aloft
and spectators search for fireflies.

Translated by: Soheil Najm

A Treatment by Music

My eye, I leave it to the walker.
Go my eye
and search the plains.
I give my ear to the stranger.
Go my ear and pick up the corner's whispers.
My mouth, I give to the whistle.
Be proud my mouth as much as you wish.
My head, I throw to the myths.
Be not so Sophist, O my head.
I make my body sleep on the dust.
Flourish, O my body, in the loftiness.
My feet relax on sponge,
my red shoes fly to the museum.

Translated by: Soheil Najm

The Big Brother

To let masks remain sacrifices and to please
the father who cleans his old whip
and asks for full rights,
he gets the Shari'a taboo out of the store
and hangs the family on the blessing wall.
Do you regret much when you took
your baptized ones back to the bath?
O, big brother,
you who bear our fetters behind you,
we revolve around you in the cells of the home,
hallow to the whip
which avenged itself
and staggered in sacred pleasure.

Translated by: Soheil Najm

Adnan al-Saiq

Born in Najaf.
Published books:
Wait For Me At Alhurriea Monument, Baghdad,
The Man Who Stayed Awake in His Delirium.

Slightly Quarrelsome Texts

Schizophrenia

In my country
fear is collecting and dividing me into:
a man writing
and another, behind my curtains,
watching me!

O

Al-Halaj[1]

Al-Halaj took me up to the highest hill in Baghdad
and let me see all its minarets, temples
and churches with bells
and pointed to me:
"Count…
How many faithful supplications
are ascending from the people's breaths?"
But no one
ascended
to give meaning to his vision
to let him see
what the dictators had done,
how the religious jurists deviated,
what the guards had done.

---

[1] Al Halaj: (c. 858 - March 26, 922) was a Persian mystic, revolutionary writer and pious teacher of Sufism, most famous for his poetry, accusation of heresy and for his execution at the orders of the Abbasid Caliph Al-Muqtadir, after a long, drawn-out investigation.

○

Al-Halaj Again

Who can save me from my affliction?
Nothing in the jubbah but him
and nothing in the jubbah but me.
I am the one
and he is the one,
how could they be united,
how could they be separated
in a moment of intoxication
between my doubts about him
and my piety?

○

Verses

Deleted
verses
yet you want your head to remain
a stone,
never to be changed through years.

○

You who are evanescent
look
how you argue God and Satan.
Is it too much to learn
how to make a dialogue with a man?

○

Neither bell
nor minaret;
O slave,
why don't
you hear
your God
in
the pipe?

○

My God
is one.
He is neither Catholic,
        nor is he Protestant,
nor is he Sunni,
nor is he Shia'a
one who distributed Him,
who interpreted Him,
who fabricated His sayings,
who classified Him
according to His faiths,
His demands,
His constitutions
and His armies
he will be the denier.

O

Four Caliphs

They left history
behind them
mouth opened,
and until now
we are drying
blood spots
for them…
O God..
how could a text
busy itself with a woman bearing firewood
and neglect those being ruled?

Translated by: Soheil Najm

Ahmed Abdussada

Born in Baghdad, 1978.
Published book:
Ash Chandliers, Baghdad 2007.

The Spindle of the Day

As usual,
the night loans its fingers
to the spindle of the day.
As usual
the day plays with its suns
that float like signboards
over the roofs of the cities.

A sun jumps like a sparrow,
embroiders the air's hair
with school ribbons,
and sweeps the pavement
with steps celebrating first passion.
A sun rushes like a stab
loading the pores of the air
with dynamite lust
to explode in the copybooks of an innocent time,
a dance for the fire ghouls.

The sun of killers could not pass easily.
It pours a galaxy of black absentmindedness
onto Buddha's pillow
and stutters the dews' dialogue with itself
in the body of the rose
as it fills the boxes of the underworld
with mothers' tears.
The sun of killers will never pass easily
on a poem's ground.

Another sun collects what scatters
from the night's buttons,

accompanies a husband leaving
his wife's milky bed with bitter eyes,
leaving the dizziness of his hot lemon
in the wilderness of her henna.
This sun spreads like a disease.
It wears a turban swollen with desert surnames,
declares a rosary from caves.
This sun could not pass easily too.
It draws from childhood gardens,
shakes hands with guns,
shackles the stature of waves
with foam virility
as it smears the nightingales' sky
with songs of mud
and sets up a kingdom of bitch dark images
on ash brains.

Many suns roll from the day's spindle…
a sun takes the moaning from,
the honey that travels between two bodies,
a sun rubs its lust with apples of loneliness,
a sun hangs around in a deserted paradise,
a sun fights for its share of the dust of the past,
a sun stands above the roses thirsty
as a scarecrow,
as sun draws its holy pulse
to strike off foggy instructions,
a sun squats in the begging bins,
a sun stretches out in the peacocks' luxury,
a sun loaded with rain drops,
a sun sweating cataracts of rust,
a sun opens a tomb for the adolescence of fertility,
a sun opens a moist cloud for the dryness of senility,
a sun crowds to reserve tickets for the absent ones,
and a sun marries absence to avoid the present.

This sun crosses the day's limits
to sink in the width of the night.
This sun remains like a mother…
is the wake of words from the inkpot of insomnia
to write down all these suns.

Ahmed Asheikh Ali

Born in Najaf, 1970.
Published book:
The Bird of Now, Baghdad 2000.

From Her Book ... Again

When:
I am her seesaw and she is my seesaw, when:
her two doves are shivering in my fingers
and her cup is full of my wine, when:
her space is diffused by my kiss
and her kiss is swimming in my space, when:
the organs startle and the violins get drunk, when:
golden deer fly in the sky of place and the epidermis
of the earth trembles, the pearl of weeping
becomes a river of firebrands! That is how
the astonishment always comes out of her book!!

O

1
The dove, when:
her song is playing with the air
of a noon without faces
…your smile
slumbers …in my heart,
slumbers like a sword,
like a sword of teardrops, it slumbers in my heart
like a teardrop in my heart,
it slumbers like a sword!

2
Another light…
the dream of the rose that has a thousand and one wings.
This rose that is dreaming,
is another light no one can reach,
washed in your teardrop, is a rose from the light
you are dreaming by!

3
What I haven't seen yet …
is your face that I always see,
your face,
that I haven't seen yet …
coming out from the shell of night,
your face that is my pearl!

4
The forest is
a cloud
and something like a blue glittering
from the bare shoulder of the river,
and the whoop of a late sun,
red
and orange
in an ivory frame.
This valuable painting
which no eye has seen,
shone in half of your vision
when your laugh quivered
like a gold sparrow
before disappearing in the forest
that no eye has seen, forever.

5
The watch on the wall
launched its seven sparrows.
The watch on the table of the bed
has been dead since yesterday,
the watch from my hand to hers…
I was late this morning.

6
She'll say,
while her teardrop is gleaming,
something about rain,
my image will be wet in her eyes

and rain will fall with the roses and the butterflies,
with the song that we would sing
calmly with a kiss…
with a kiss, the song, the butterflies and the roses,
rain will fall heavy this morning!

7
I'll reach late,
twenty years will precede me to her.
My heart will beat.
I'll say something about the seven sparrows of the watch,
about my hand and hers,
how so much rain perplexes my eyes,
about a forgotten kiss in a song.
We would sing calmly as we pass the day
if the figure of a watch had died twenty years ago.

8
Her teardrop, that is gleaming,
is a song about rain,
and about a kiss,
an old song about her and me,
an old song
we couldn't remember exactly,
a song nobody sang about the watch,
from my hand to hers

9
What will I say?
I was late this morning,
I was late twenty years this morning!

Translated by: Soheil Najm

Ahmed Adam

Born in Karballa, 1973
Killed by terrorists in Baghdad, 2005.

The Guide to the Window

Who can imagine being a day?
Repeating oneself after a night of sleep
and being conscious of the repetition?
Do you know…
why the man grows older but his hair never becomes grey?
Am I your night?
Since the first year…
maybe…
I remember nothing but my whimper,
shining from a timid lantern
and I repeat all that the hours brought down
with grief…
and unbearable desire…
no…
do I love you?
Why should I reveal the secret of your teardrop
to a migrating bird?
It returns not.
Maybe.
And who can imagine that they are a day?
I know not?
Who can shine without the night?

Brightly, you deny the morning
and peel the night
from it's fright
and the fear of its bells
and for a heart that waves
with a stumbling hand,
you spread daffodils that never exist.
There is no one but you…

you are bright
and without sleep you shine.
I love you… do you love?
Why then?
Your night shivers and with me you shine.

Translated by: Sadek R. Mohammed

Formations

(1)
Apologetically, I write my death,
on a plain piece of paper,
in a word, which is the last that is left for me.
(I love you).

(2)
So ...
there is no problem in this disorder,
because you slowly lifted your hand off this world.

(3)
How clever seems this moon!
It unveils its magnificence at night,
when the sun is in its cottage.
Only lovers
notice this.

(4)
I burned the forests of the world with my heart
and ran away
like a child who fears fire.

(5)
Because I was afraid that streets might be forgotten,
I hired a pauper.

(6)
Every time I open my eyes
I find the wolf still eating me.

(7)
Because I lean not against a wall,
I have become old.

(8)
When they fired,
the most delicate of my friends
was the first to hit me.

(9)
O houses!
Be not more compassionate.
We want to take refuge in hotels.

Translated by: Dr. Sadek R. Mohammed

Ahmed Sadawi
Born in 1973.
Published books:
The Beautiful Country, Baghdad 2004,
The Festival of Bad Expectations, Madrid 2000.

Who Am I This Year?

1
I'll be the driver of the old queen
when she goes to buy vegetables
and fish!
Or when she forgets, because of her senility,
and shouts for the fall of the monarchy.

2
I'll be always the friend of the hero
when the burden of the truth and its light
are cast only on him!
That is why I have the freedom of harmless
entering and going
from the tales.

3
I'll never be Jesus
nor Judas,
neither God nor his faithful angel.
I'll never be the damned tree
nor whoever touches it.
I'll be the one who thought about this story
then slept on the pillow of eternity.

4
I'll be the orchard keeper who is not in his orchard,
and the writer who is not in his book,
the sleeper in the beds of other men's wives,
which are empty of the wives
and full with the scents of the others.
I'll be the muezzin

who is not in his mosque
and the prayer in the revel of the night,
I'll be just a remote light
but not a star.

5
I'll be a chocolate skeleton,
not just a slim person.
I'll be a big delicious steak,
and a spiritual drink
but not rain with a taste of logic.

6
I'll be feast clothes
that are worn all year,
I'll be a colored sock
on a leg of a girl,
not on a leg of a government officer,
a paper tie that burns
in the corridors of the state,
a winter jacket from the fishermen nets,
a hat woven from a horse tail,
a glove to catch clouds
not knowing the hand in it.

7
I'll be the water in the week
and the stick in the year,
the night in the wall
and the idea in the bed
but I'll never be
that man standing in the rain
waiting for a taxi since morning.

8
I'll be the besieged lieutenant
in the ministry of defense
but not the military statement.

So not to be the walls of the city themselves
I'll be bad paint for them.
I'll be the war that ends everyday,
I'll be the saved soldier
believing in a fable
that the war takes only the dead.

9
I'll be the seesaw,
even when there are no children,
a balloon, even when there is no pin.
I'll be a postponed fate
because this is better than
no fate.
I'll be an aspirin tablet
because this is better than
a kiss on the head.

10
I'll be bread in front of the books
and water in front of the words,
a crowd of sweepers, trees, streets
and another town where tourists enjoy
a lovely time.

11
I'll be a fat sparrow
that doesn't like to fly
but works as a keeper
for the nests of immigrant
birds.

Translated by: Soheil Najm

Akeel Ali

Born in Nasiria, 1949.
Published books:
Gardens of Adam, Alribat 1992.
Another Bird Vanishes, Paris 1992.

A Body That Speaks by Its Limbs

I am a body that speaks by its limbs,

for courage I take the flowers
of whomever I love.

I stand up and sing the blood
of a common mouth.

I am the softness of the depths
before your fingers' virgin beats.

I want you because of the child
that reflects its turn in the mirror.

I want you

for this never-tiring fondness

for what we've been through

and what we await.

I want you because of this sea
that devours everything

and will never spare me.

Translated by: Dr. Sadek R. Mohammed

Star

There is a star, there, that commiserates with my unruliness,
and pats the illusions from which I suffer.

There is a star, there, that commiserates with my screams

before my very eyes.

I shall recite the poems of the star.

Translated by: Dr. Sadek R. Mohammed

Blood of Desire

What is breaking my heart is the blood of extinguished desire,
the clamor of the clouds that examine themselves attentively
in the mask of my boredom and the echoes of my memory.

My dream is mysterious and was tarnished by the blood of poverty.

Translated by: Dr. Sadek R.Mohammed

Ali Abdulameer

Born In Babel, 1955.
Published Books:
Two Hands Referring to the Idea of Pain. Baghdad, 1993,
Take the Songs as a Praise For Your Absence. Beirut, 1996,
Chapters in Contemporary Music.

Vanishing Country

The rain falls on terrified vehicles.
The rain is cold on corpses in the vehicles.
The rain falls on the black flags of the Iraqis.
The rain falls on their war.
The rain is in its balconies.
The rain falls in ditches in the far dust.
The rain falls on the soldier's helmet when he shoots.
The rain fills his mouth when he is dead.
The rain falls on my head when I bury my dreams.
Rain fills the vehicles of the murdered.
Rain falls on my city,
on my balconies that were dry
and my withered evenings.
Rain falls on fast vehicles.
Rain falls on corpses in the vehicles.
Rain fills the soldier's helmet
and mud fills the country's balconies.

7th of March 2003
Amman

Translated by: Soheil Najm

There Were Roses Around

There was a life though it was in the wars' dregs.
There was his hand and he was happy with the grass on his shirt.
There was pleasure though it was jumping among traps.
There was a city.
There were roses flourishing on our hands.
No more roses around now.
No woman's hand can be tender, a smiling tomorrow.

Translated by: Soheil Najm

Tomorrow Is Expelled From Our Balconies

1
Every thing is enrolled in his temper:
Distance will launch its doves to the dust
and alienation will put its stone in the mouth of the stranger.
Every melody calms.
What are written dreams in far away regions
where no heart can shrink,
where disaster can drink coffee in the houses?

2
Priests of ruin,
guardians of dream in Nostalgia Valley
make melody of speech,
throw away tomorrow from our balconies
and plant it in broken jars.

Translated by: Soheil Najm

Ali Habash

Born in Baghdad, 1956.
Published book:
Years Without Cause, Tunisia, 2001.

A Second Rate Future

At the top of the page in the street…there are inverted sentences
and necks turned around by dinars.
Despair hides in the airports, and near The Martyrs Bridge
a family stumbles, victims like everything that fills
the mother's bag…

I enter the country with a ticket.
It is the Baghdadi Museum or prisoners of war
mistaking their homeland…
I remember: the bus was passing by
and I was smartly crossing Rimbaud[1]
and The Martyrs into my lesson's journey…
Shelters were not my dreams
and the ration card was farther away than the bomb…
O World, your fangs decimated the hospital
and your children are multiplying on the pavement.

What is left for us…?
At last I have seen my life in the museum
without the beggars.
They are dead like weapons.
The child is puzzled. He stumbles upon the truth
and the mother cannot digest mysteries.
She talks to me about the price of gold today.
Poetry negotiates with me in chimneys…
O Mother, necessity has its own sorrows…

A naked dancer stops me.
Desire wounds the place always.
They are without memories cheerfully gnawing
bits of dust all day and do not know war.
If I were one of them…?

A bullet would be a funny idea
and homeland would be mere ink on paper…
Al-Rusafi[2] is still solemnly standing in the middle of the problem,
and airplanes follow me in news bulletins every day.
No discipline can see a lifetime…
Dreams retreat like an army.
They do not reach the Al-Karkh side and do not listen to darkness.
I, alone, rush pell-mell with the mountain.
The teeth of the day have fallen beside me.
I go out to a lofty threshold called Al-Rasheed Street.
Khaki still colors my country's garages…
At the bottom of a lifetime falls Al-Zawra park.[3]
Between my dreams and tea, mothers throng towards Najaf[4]…
Popcorn bags remind me of metal money
and the old man who plays desert tunes for a dinar…

Humiliation is breathing!
Children's trifling is a second-rate future.
The lion paces in the flat bread.
Splinters reach the zoo!
Who would hang washing on a clothesline?
Mothers or Sweden? Planes are held up by dollars.
Our contagious diseases make picnics in resumes only.
In Al-Zawra the void was larger than my life.

For the first time I see the palm trees massacred.
How can I translate this war to money mongers,
to my brother who always desires the future,
and I master nothing of Arabic except its wailing,
and two children who slipped through negative sentences?

My language tries to digest the alleyway
and move away from forty wolves smiling in newspapers and corpses…
I remember the double-decker bus as it slips to me into bed…
They have sold it with the junk in Al-Maidan Square[5].
My day decays regularly
at nine sharp.
Barbed wire cuts through the house…I run into a cup of tea…

I open a window; no breeze answers my greeting.
A pointer drags the family to the roofs…
Where are you heading, O country?
"Born in Baghdad and will die in it."[6]
For the first time, poetry beguiles the truth and comes out victorious.
The grave competes with ambulances.

I declare my defeat in front of the glass.
In the house of millions for pain,
I wrote: *dreams were demobilized from the army.*
Poetry errs in prosody
and bedrooms are scratched every day in courts…
Poetry trades me for dams!
Yesterday I saw a dam called traveling abroad.
Weeping is approaching the bus.

My purse kicks me to the market…
Father I shall go to hell with them.
In the grocery market the mademoiselle's flesh was terrifying men
Her blood kicked beside me.
I desired her smiling stocking and the leg that tears the cloth.
Then I remember the fangs of the house
and the ice that died in the deepfreeze.
At the top of her face there are wrinkles that rip the future…

Father, water does not reach the washbasin.
These are the lame presents of summer.
Numbness traverses the clock; it rises up towards the buildings
and the colonel redeems his glories with tea and empty bottles.
The cup of tea breathes in the elevator
between her make-up and the floors numbers.
Make-up is the sign of anxiety in the face…
With a dull defeat, he speaks to me about poetry as if I were a resume.
He sums up the poets by a coffeehouse
and the ones slain by northern Europe.

They bandage the country with letters and phone calls…
Across the continent he talks to me about Al-Waziriyah[7]
and inhales the bridges.
He writes: *London is seven days in my life.*
And near the traffic lights a child buys his dreams by begging…
Betrayals thrive in places of exile.

Baghdad, 1/6/1999

[1] The French poet Arthur Rimbaud.
[2] The Iraqi poet Ma'aroof Al-Rusafi.
[3] A park in Baghdad.
[4] An Iraqi city where there is the largest cemetery in the world.
[5] A garage in Baghdad.
[6] Quoted from the Iraqi poet Salman Dawood Mohammed.
[7] A district in Baghdad.

Translated by: Dr. Sadek R. Mohammed

Ali al-Imarah

Born in Basra, 1970.
Published books:
Running After a Standing Thing, Basra 1998,
Empty Places, Basra 1998.

Difficulty

A vast country
and a small heart.
How difficult nostalgia is!
Black ink
and a black piece of paper.
How difficult writing is!

Translated by: Dr. Sadek R. Mohammed

Grandchildren

What shall we leave behind
for our grandchildren
if we don't give them a chance
to be grandchildren?

Translated by: Dr. Sadek R. Mohammed

Helmet

This city looks like a helmet.
When we put it on our heads,
its top seems clear
and when we take it off, its dark,
fearful bottom becomes clear.
It is our fate — we veterans —
to fill the bottom with our heads
so that the top of the city becomes clear.

Translated by: Dr. Sadek R. Mohammed

Amal al-Jubouri
Born in Baghdad.
Published books:
Wine of Wounds, Baghdad, 1986,
Set Me Free Oh Words, Amman, 1994,
For You This Body I Am Not Afraid, Beirut, 1999.

The Veil of Eve

Eve has two tongues and four lips.
Two lips live in the light
and two in the darkness.
In the light they are elongated like the equator.
In the darkness they react like a bamboo column.
Her first tongue speaks many languages,
and her second tongue can speak just one.

Translated by: Soheil Najm

The Veil of Adam

When God withdrew from Mary's body,
he left scars,
mines and roses.
Yet He created contrast for her—
two tongues.
The first lives in the light uncovering its mines
and the other lives in the darkness catching the mines
pleased by death's agony.

Roses were dispersed at the gate of the cave.

Translated by: Soheil Najm

Baqir Sahib
Born in Simawa.
Published book:
Daily Birds, Baghdad, 1999.

A Wolf Without Prey

I left.
I have no choice but to be
a wolf of words.
Neither sullen houses
will tame me,
nor my wife's advice
to come back early.
Bearing baskets of drowsiness
O, night of the city,
squat on a TV screen
we watch the world's wars
and the sad trains of soldiers.

Go you then to propagate
with barking dogs,
give birth to the foundling day.
O, wolf of words
there are no signs
for your coagulated dreams
on the trees of years
wrapped in blankets,
yet there are gazelles
leaping
when they see
a creature —
its upper half of words
and lower half
two crossed lines.

Here you have to
remain chasing
and be chased,
writing your poems
in the newspapers of the deserts
that slip like the crescent moon
on the night of Eid,
and plant your seeds
in an old hole
deserted by water,
seeking a young tree.

O, wolf of words,
neither the graveyard wall nor the chicken farm
will bridle your deserts.
There is no she-wolf
to create a progeny camp,
O, creature
whose upper half is of words
and lower half is two lines,
you have only
to pick up the female fire
from the word's ribs,
only to pierce a hole
in the eternal darkness
as the final curtain
drops.

Pick up the female glow
without looking at the desert screen.
Crow memory,
Abel eyes,
the first grave,
Irem with columns,
the ship,
the flood,
the channels of love
and the rat's eyes.

O, globe tubercular
with human greed,
O, wolf of words,
you left
and left,
yet the stations of the circles
are without stations.

April, 1994

Basim al-Murabi
Born in Diwania, 1960.
Published books:
The Devoid of Flower, London, 1988,
Three Collections, Beirut, 1997,
The Bitter Land, Beirut, 1998.

The Days of the Tiger

In the vacuum of the cage he drinks,
as the tiger lets his eyes wander with his dreams,
weaving from his tormented days
a bridge
to his hidden forests.

He rubs his memory,
smelling the wild, recalling killed times
in a mirror mounted by wrinkles.

The tiger
in his wounded dreams
is measuring the cage
as a dry moon
measures space.

The days of the tiger
are shrinking cages
nothing penetrating them but waiting.
Every day
he cancels the sun on the wall
when his eyes dwell,
in flame.
Rivers,
pastures,
provinces and planets
become as near as a closed eye to his awakening.

Translated by: Soheil Najm

Air of the Exile

O, my daughter,
this is the air of the exile.
It has neither color
nor taste nor smell.
A merciless air,
its sky is less blue
and more silence.
But the earth here
is earth that sinks
in the sweat of our hearts.
Lightly it goes, like a shadow.
Stretch tight your steps
O, my daughter.
The earth is solid,
baked by our dreams
for a long time.

The horizon is moved by
the blowing of our eyes
and your fathers'
shoulders are weighing
the night and the day.

Air of the exile is mute.
We learned to measure
by its silence
our words…

Translated by: Soheil Najm

A Poet in Exile

I ask you poet:
where is your country?

O

Clouds erase a teardrop
or fasten it like a dot above a letter.
I ask you poet,
when seven vultures augment your power
to complete your legend —
a fog of mystery wraps your eyes,
you say ... you hid it in a teardrop,
you hid it in a rose under your shirt—
I ask you poet
where is your mirror?
You point a finger home,
to the horizon of the soul.

O

And gold is the filing of silence,
and like a fortune-teller who has gold,
mirrors and a mask,
you affirm
the teardrop's grimace
is a never lying mirror.

Translated by: Soheil Najm

Basim Furat

Born in Najaf 1967.
Published books:
The Tougher Cooing, Madrid, 1999,
Autumn of the Minarets, Amman, 2002.

Man of Blood

With chains of indignity
and stumbling steps
he heads to the glory
he built from
mothers' weeping
and orphans' tears.

His breakfast is blood,
his dinner is blood,
his supper is blood.
His drink is a wail of a widow;
and wars are his joy.
His hobbies are palaces
and mass graves.

This man of blood
with his chains
now needs only
a piper
to play his pipe.

Translated by: Soheil Najm

Life Runs Wherever You Catch It

O, women of Babylon,
O, granddaughters of hurt,
place the wind in Procession Street,
and hang the wail on Ishtar's roads.
Here darkness climbs the seasons:
Hussein[1] has died.
Fill evenings with incense,
go through his youth,
stand over his bier,
disperse femininity,
let candles bleed and burn.
On language let your weeping extend.

I said to him;
"Life runs wherever you catch it
and wherever you leave your valor
to dissolve is a banquet for the soil,
do not boast of your revenge,
since you shut your book to everyone."

O, girls of Babylon;
Hussein has died.
Let us count the orchards on his shirt,
the longing of the doves
and all the letters the bombardment
forgot.
Let us count too
his father's wisdom under autumn's control
and his date palms,
and let us call out through the land:
Hussein has died!

You distributed the dawn to us
and divided the day with us,
you fed us directions
and split dryness to create rain,
you led perplexity
to a certain pasture

that spread flowers and kisses
over our weeping
and when fear weighed on our shoulders
you disposed of our stumbles.
How then…
did you let absence
lessen your glamour in us?
Please mind not
our tears when they inscribe:
Hussein
Has died…

1. Poet's note: Hussein is my cousin who could not escape the hand of death unleashed in the streets of Iraq, September 2006.

Translated by: Soheil Najm

Delawar Qaradaghi

Born in Suleimania, 1963.
Published books:
A Statue From Rain,
Ismaeel Birds,
Completely Naked Like Water, Damascus, 1999.

Completely Naked Like Water

I stayed under the debris.
When I came, the night building half-lit
clung to the braids of space
like a strange snowflake
afraid of the desert sorrows,
shamed before the rage of the mountains.
As I raised my head the holy books
collected the lonely prophet's jubbahs,[1]
their glasses and sticks.
Yet the broker of the phantom countries
devoured them. And I stayed.
I stayed like a sparrow, on the alert, at sunset
one December evening.
I stayed like a guilty old highwayman.
My horse is occupied with itself and me
and a forest heavily armed with mirrors.
I stayed like an incomplete equation.
On the blackboard of the school
a confused teacher left me
to the guesses of gray classes.
I stayed like a coverless copybook of thirty pages.
A lazy child left me at the dying shelves
of oblivion.
I stayed alone like a stabbed spike
drowned in longing,
rainy years.
I stayed like a disappointed disciple.
I stayed like a letter fallen from a mouth
of a rash lover.

[1.] A Jubbah is a long, often white, garment or robe worn by men.

I stayed alone like unquenched thirst.
I stayed alone like the hymns of martyred doves
when songs change into water in their throats,
I stayed like the lamp posts of my district, Alazab,
I and my horse that is occupied with itself,
and a sky pregnant with glassy clouds.
These men were having bread and pearls
for breakfast mornings
and were gathering evenings:
They blew up as our eye lanterns dimmed
and our still green hopes were gnawed away.
O, my beautiful broken horse,
I am neighing to see you
and I am writing poetry so you will hear me.
They took us to visit the springs of adultery
then left, observing the cooing and flattery!
I and my horse that is occupied with itself
and a room in the space of a poem.
There, naked like water
pretending to be dumb against the wounds
eagerly contemplated the process of the light,
that room was the center of the universe.
The charm of the forests runs
in the soul of a bottomless desert
as clouds ride wooden winds.
Come and settle here.
Always here, in this room,
strange and naked like the water
they allocate love
and protect us.
Here is the center of the universe,
here…always,
two strangers shivering from cold like water
return to the spring
raising their hands from time to time
greeting us …
here…always…here…

ignorant…naked like water.
They were dusting themselves
from the dust of the rocks' doubt
and were generous to the coast's love.
This room was the center of the universe…
two strangers…
silent …generous…naked like water.
They were always busy with our troubles.

Translated from Kurdish by: Azad Barazanji
Translated from Arabic by: Soheil Najm

Faliha Hassan
Born in Najaf, 1967.
Published Books:
Even After a While.
Because I Am a Girl,
A Visit to the Shadow Museum

On the Fringe of the War

"Those are stars,"
says the child,
as airplanes tear up the face of the sky.
"Before two wars," his sister says,
"I used to rest my head
upon his kind bosom.
I don't remember how we
found the bones of the murdered one.
My father
was defending us on this mirage-territory
asking a shadow who it belonged to originally?"

The ash women cry,
"These are the portents of those lost
in the darkness of the prisons."
One of them calls for help,
"I didn't find him.
He left without a helmet,
and nothing distinguishes him
but his heart.
He was like my country
too big to be carried.
They returned many corpses
but not his."
"These are the marks of a faded morning,"
says the woman who, still
tidying the bed blankets,
dreams he may come in one longing night,
light a match,
pull the covers from her bed.

"These are the memories of past years,"
says one who has just come.
"To whom has my age been sold as wood fire
for a fire that has raged for twenty-three years
without ending?
These are mirrors for my hollow life."

Birds cry as they follow an Apache squadron,
"Where are the windows?
Where are the windows?
We want windows!"

Translated by: Soheil Najm

Hadi al-Husseiny

Born in Baghdad.
Published book:
The Fog of the Shrines.

Fog of Graves

Among columns of fog
graves disappear.
Farewells emerge suddenly.
There is no movement but moaning
marginalized in the soul,
rising on
the margin of pain
under the suns
of dark rivers.
Tears are compelled
to hide
and departure comes to pass
burdened by the collapse of hope.

O

Far away from the date palms
near agonized fences
I release the flocks
of sighs
roosting
on my chest.
In my thin body
filled with loss,
protected by the fog,
just after sunset fades
melted by nightfall,
exile goes away
leaving behind
queues of graves.

○

Some days
I enter cities
gasping from strikes of war,
only to leave hurriedly
letting the date palms
lie in their shadows
to rest from standing.

○

Some days
I request wounds of live bodies—
the paradox of the desert,
with its dark odor
that never feels pain
unless after death.

○

I am shocked by this stupidity
and quickly
prepare to leave
even as
my farewell is disappearing
behind fog columns.

Translated by: Soheil Najm

Haider al-Ka'abi

Born in Basra, 1954.
Published book:
Bombardment, Damascus 1998

The Sword

The handgrip of the sword
is condemned
not because killing
is banned,
but because the one who
holds the sword
is a coward.

Basra, 1973

Translated by: Dr. Sadek R. Mohammed

The Body Call

Two teardrops guard the breast lilies.
Two drops of wax in sinful orange
gruff in clothes and chummy accent.
O what fear the maid has as she takes refuge in hand
and slips the bread bundle away, when two buds
lisp "r" within her.
They are warm like a domestic cat
and they shiver.

Basra, 1981

Translated by: Dr. Sadek R. Mohammed

Hameed Qassim

Born in Baghdad, 1954.
Published books:
First Statement For the Old Childhood. (A Novel), Baghdad, 1983.
Requiem of the Aged Childhood, (Poems), Baghdad 1984,
There Is No Air, (Poems), Shariqeh, 2000,
This Is Also True, (Poems), Beirut, 2007.

True Nature

I think about you—

I think about you
more than a ray of sunlight
in a glass of cold water,
and I look
at my life
like a shirt thrown on a bed.

Blood—
The old clouds
will go away…and may be back,
the heavy air…waving to them,
carrying from them nothing
to the smell of blood.
How many times should I do this?
Either blood… or risk!
What shall I do with
all these questions alone?
What shall I do with all
this blood that floods the plains?
What shall I do with these tears
that drench my handkerchiefs?
There is always blood …
and if not,
there is a smell that leads to it!

A wish—
I want to breathe…
but the air hurts me.

True Nature—
O, God…
the wide scene of life
is a prejudiced mixture…!
O, God…
Whenever I close my eyes
I see my life…
baptized over an old fire!

Weep—
A line of tears
leaks from the cars
as they pass quickly by
and in their depths
women in black sit.
It is a prolonged weeping
on endless roads.

Translated by: Soheil Najm

Hanadi al-Nassar
Born in Nsiria, 1975.

A Wheat Bird

I look at it.
While I am in the city's cage,
I look at it,
when it is in heaven's cage,
I look at it,
when it is near me,
I listen to its look,
I listen to the wing's touch,
I listen to the feathers' smell,
I escort it on the way,
to the house cage.
I look at it
as it walks besides me.
We enter a golden cage,
larger than this world.
I look at it
in the cage,
as it tills its garden,
waters it,
and plants it
with wheat like embers.
I look at it
when it is far from me.
I set my sparrows
free
towards it,
towards its shoulders.
I look at it.
and I wait…
every night,
I remember a dove,
and my bird
returns
carrying with it

the wheat
and the sparrows.
It enters my cage so that I lock
behind a wheat bird.
My bird
is the hawk
that writes its never sleeping poem.

Translated by: Dr. Sadek R. Mohammed

Ghosts in a Mass Grave

Alone,
the illuminating lover
picks out pairs
from us
in the dimness of fear
for the ship in the land of the flood.

☉

A skull in a burial ground,
a rabid dog
escaping to a rat's hole.

☉

Ghosts prepare themselves
for traps.
They sniff.
They howl
and show their fangs and bite.

☉

A big skull —
the world is a ghosts' pomegranate.
Numerous animals
are besieged by its rind.

☉

This is a balance
between the blind and those who see.

O

A mass grave
that contains the hand bones,
the feet,
the teeth —
O what ash!
Cages are besieging us.

O

They bark
and roam in the world's pomegranate.

O

Trapped ghosts
meander in our lives.

O

Black words
buried the white bones.

O

A mass pomegranate,
an open grave
a frantic fugitive
blew up my slain country.

O
A mass grave
that contains a skull—
its jaws are biting the sky.

○

Ghosts alone
in their traps pick us off
one by one
to return to the dust pit.

Translated by: Dr. Sadek R. Mohammed

Hashem Shafeeq

Born in Falujah, 1955.
Published books:
Amiable Poems, Baghdad, 1978,
House Moons, Damascus, 1980,
An Apparition From Pottery, Beirut, 1991.

The Handkerchief

There is a handkerchief
floating in the air like a cloud,
white in color… embroidered
with threads of pure gold,

It falls down in my hand.
I smell it…
My mother's fragrance is in it.
I rub it…
Bread and tea flowers fall from it,
and when I knot it around a Mecca pebble
or around blue and indigo stones,
it protects me from an aftermath
and turns me into diverse clouds.
There is a handkerchief floating
like a breath of air.
It stirs my hair
and covers me with river slight whiffs.

Translated by: Dr. Sadek R. Mohammed

The Needle

She sat darning her sock,
the skirt,
and withered curtains.
She drank her coffee in the shadow
and looked outside
to examine the borders of space.
She saw a vast desert
being torn like a dress.
She turned her needle until
they twinkled in the corners
and started darning the vast tear
in the body of the desert.

Translated by: Dr. Sadek R. Mohammed

Husein Ali Yunis

Born in Baghdad 1967.
Published book:
Tales and Bitterness, Colon 2005.

Poem

In the past
there was one Don Quixote,
only one Don Quixote,
tormented by imagination.
But now all of us are Don Quixotes.
Don Quixote has drawn us in
and we cannot tell if we are one Don Quixote
or a limitless number of Don Quixotes.

Poem

Shedding too many tears
only the knights of time
are standing near the gates.

Poem

Time floods
like a fish
out of a waterfall.

Translated by: Soheil Najm

The Depression Of Enkidu[1]

I am sitting now in the house.
This is the day Babel will be rebuilt.
All the people are at home
rebuilding their houses.
Flagstones are ruined because of the heat.
Walls are peeled.
Spiders have been spreading
their gleaming threads
in dusty corners for a long time.
What can a man do on such a dusty day?
It makes one feel the heaviness
of the existence, the burden.
The rotten Babel that had no consistency
doesn't amaze me these days...
nor do the days in the heart of this city
that is taking shape, wet and rotten.

I have left my memory wandering
in city delights.
In the dark, a heavy fan
is moving very slowly,
as if existence has crystallized,
intensified.

[1] Enkidu was the friend of Gilgamesh in the epic of Gilgamesh.

Translated by: Soheil Najm

Jalal Zangabadi
Born in Zangabad, Diyala, 1952.

In a Disastrous Map

Wherever the Swastika glitters,
wars and black markets reproduce.
All smiles, daily bread
and our water supply will be lost.
Wives, spinsters, widows, maids
and bereaved children
become ghosts and surround my future.
They bleed, withered, wailing and moaning
until their last breath stiffens in grief
and in spite of the spider of a bank note
some of them sew remaining slim hope
in an endless lament, a map of bereavement
under a heap of the trash of treason
in my country which has not
shone above me for ages…

Translated by: Soheil Najm

What an Ignoramus Was I!

What an ignoramus was I
when I thought that my heart was made of iron..!
I didn't know
your heart could magnetize it
make me suddenly a beggar
in the presence of the Sultan
shaking like the tears of a bereaved child,
who after turning his eyelashes
to the sun
still sows his soul
and gets no fruit.

Translated by: Soheil Najm

My Question Invades Me

On the banks of rivers,
on the trunks of trees,
on the walls of caves,
on stones
and on carpets and on fences,
didn't my shadow eternal
fade with all my truths and aberrations?!
And now
do not five thousand of me die
of starving every day,
yet I don't care?!

Translated by: Soheil Najm

Kadhim al-Hajaj

Born in Basra, 1946.
Published books:
At Last Shahrayar Talked, Baghdad, 1976.
Basrian Rhymes, Baghdad, 1990.

Suleiman al-Halabi[1]

Gaza is the beginning;
the sea does not end nearby,
but begins
from all ends.
The Bedouins collect their things.
An oasis disappears in the mirage.
Gaza is promised now to the night:
to the invaders
or to a wanderer surrounded by wolves!

〇

Our guest loves silence,
but he told me
—in the morning—
"The birds that do not travel
do not deserve wings!"

〇

The sea is born of a cloud
as war is born
of pride!
Like this, the Bedouins walk out,
cannot peddle goods
in empty shops.
O Suleiman!
To know a people
it suffices to look at their shops.
Do the poor buy?

O

Egypt closed its districts,
Suleiman,
and the pavement was overcrowded
with strangers.
The streets called for prayer:
God is…
G…
…reat…
When you performed ablution,
you turned your face east to
…The Levant.

[1] Suleiman Al-halabi (also known as Soleyman El-Halaby): (1777-1800) was a Syrian student who assassinated the French general Jean Baptiste Kléber. He was executed by impalement.

Translated by: Dr. Sadek R. Mohammed

The Wedding Ceremony of Ali Bin Mohammed[1]

Hungrily, we stopped at an oasis.
We did not eat dates lest the Bedouins
tell their master's soldiers or shout.
The road to your house was wide-awake with soldiers.
Let them not hear your breathing and open not your door,
and smile not in the darkness; the soldiers might see your teeth.
Praise not God lest the soldiers hear the sound of your prayer!
If anyone of you knocks at my door,
I will feed him half of my heart, and make of the other half
a mattress for him to sleep on.
You blamed me and my color was not enough intercession for you.
No suns have scorched me as they have scorched your face
and you were not nourished by my mother's breast
when you were young.
But they have united our hearts in abhorrence of shackles.
If you are one of us then set out,
but if you are not then follow the caravan
behind pregnant women.

O

"And captive women passed by."
And I dyed my hands with the color of my cheeks and waited,
and let my hair loose to my knees as you told me,
and I consulted women about the color of the gauzy fabric
I should wear. They said wear the color of his eyes.
They said 'wear' and I shivered
as the color of your eyes is the color of mourning.
And they beat drums like the sound of wailing
so my tent—by your eyes— swirled me and I fell back
and they passed by my door:

Soldiers
      and captives

           soldiers

               and captives

                  soldiers

and God
make you travel headless by night to him.

[1] Ali Bin Mohamed is the leader of the famous Negro Revolution in Basra.

Translated by: Dr. Sadek R. Mohammed

Khazaal al-Majidi

Born in Baghdad, 1956.
Published Books:
The Songs of Israphel, Baghdad 1978.
A Contrary Physics, Baghdad 1998.

The Amulet of the Hot Woman

She knocked
and sang,
thus the house sang.
She swirled and tumbled,
thus fire erupted.
By Allah, O star of the night, wake up!
And get intoxicated with us by her hot wine.

Translated by: Dr. Sadek R. Mohammed

The Talisman of the Mouth — the Wound

This mouth
is an old wound in the prophet body
or in the devil body.
When will our wound heal?
When will it forgive?
When will time bury
the far-off cave and the drunken boat?

Translated by: Dr. Sadek R. Mohammed

The Amulet of Fire

And you discovered the fire around you
but you discovered not the fire within you
which is still flaring up
when you sleep and when you wake.
You are still dipping your limbs in it
and you are still flying to your first wine
to ignite your drunken days
and on grass you lie down and crawl.

Translated by: Dr. Sadek R. Mohammed

Khalil al-Asadi

Born in Baghdad, 1950.
Published books:
Primitive Hymns, Baghdad, 1978.
The Pipe of the Time, Baghdad, 2000.
And Your Perfume Remains in the Place, Baghdad, 2005.

Fear

The intention is

not to call the sky a country,

to call prisons houses,

to take refuge in a child's rings

and a lady's mirror

and shout:

Cool down.

Translated by: Dr. Sadek R. Mohammed

The Intention

Then,
this was the intention:
to build myself a wind house
and not reside in it,
to change the old directions
but not dive into my own direction,
to build some ships
but not to sail in these ships,
to call childhood my weapons
without knowing the intention,
to surpass all small kings
and remain without a kingdom.

Translated by: Dr. Sadek R. Mohammed

Khalid al-Ma'ali

Born in Samawa, 1956.
Published books:
Eyes Thought of Us, London 1999.
Residence in the Open, Colon 2006.

Speech

Nothing hears me in the light
save the letters I use to write my name,
In the corners of the forest I am the only tenant.
I distinguish the whining of trees from other sounds.
I swap various forms with my shadows
and grant my dreams everlasting dryness
so I can strike one rock against another.
This is my great fire.
I burn my daydreams in order to sleep,
to halt the march of memories behind me.
My moment of death is near.
It lives within me.
I exchange mute words with it,
words my tongue trifles with.
If I thought of anything but this
I would prepare queues of letters
beginning with "no"
so I would say nothing.

1988

Translated by: Dr. Sadek R. Mohammed

My Setback Is Incessant

My setback is incessant
without water and without a wall,
its memories are in the balance.
Others knew this and I knew
the meaning of sitting without rhyme.

The most beautiful thing is balance.
Of its dreams we write a book.
We justify the wind
and reap the harvest.

An end yesterday.
Nothing present but a leaf.
So we knew autumn
without a need for this smoke.
You have to think of ash
when mistakes arrive constantly.

Without meaning
I had a cup
in which words woke up.

1985

Translated by: Dr. Sadek R. Mohammed

Lateef Helmet
Born in Kirkuk 1947.
Published books:
Allah and Our Small City,
The Braids of That Girl Are My Tent Summer and Winter,
The Good Word Is a Rose.

The Storm

Even the storm is a criminal,
for many times it broke the boughs of the trees,
for many times it tore the bodies of the children,
for many times it drove away the birds out of the woods.
Even the storm is a criminal
for many times it filled the eyes of the city
with dust and fog.
Even the storm is a criminal.
We will hang the storm someday.

Translated from Kurdish into Arabic by: Abdullah Tahir al Baranzanji
Translated from Arabic into English by: Soheil Najm

Home

When they came
they thought that my home
was a beautiful naked woman
they could take to any toilet they wished,
to any brothel they wished.
They thought my home was a naked woman
who loved rings and bracelets,
and could be enticed by a necklace and two combs.
They didn't know that it was a holy place
surrounded by thousands of lovers.

Translated from Kurdish into Arabic by: Abdullah Tahir al – Baranzanji
Translated from Arabic into English by: Soheil Najm

You Are in My Heart

Half of my heart is love
and the other is poetry.
Yet you understand neither poetry
nor love.
When I am behind any window
shut or open,
I look for you
but you are always
in my heart.

Translated from Kurdish into Arabic by: Abdullah Tahir al – Baranzanji
Translated from Arabic into English by: Soheil Najm

Sugar

God revolted against the sea
and turned it into snow,
I revolted against my heart
and turned it into poetry
and poetry revolted against the word
and turned it into sugar.

Translated from Kurdish into Arabic by: Abdullah Tahir al – Baranzanji
Translated from Arabic into English by: Soheil Najm

Mohammed Mazloom

Born in Baghdad, 1963.
Published books:
Commissions Never To Be Stipulated, Beirut, 1992,
The Delayed Passing Through the Mirrors of Suspicions, Beirut ,1994,
The Sleeper and His Autobiography of Wars, Beirut, 1998.

Anabasis

The ancient, tired, barbarians were defeated
but too much death remained after their fall.
They crossed into the shadows without
pavement or a guide!

They were defeated —
flags were colored by the bleeding eyes of their armies,
their own eyes blurred like the eyes of those killed,
a deviation of massacre.

They planted their sky with trees, like a forest of swords
which gleam at sunset
but do not pray for eclipse.

And so the sky was for them abandoned,
like the sands of Ur[1] or like feasts
after all guests have fled,
and more guests have arrived.

The vanquished left,
shall we then end our story?

There were newcomers
reviewing a map for sleeping awakened by the didactic
of its story.

The barbarians I knew had already passed
over the old maps, over ruin here, there!

They scattered, and their profiles hid
a paradise of chaos.

And death commenced to menstruate
out of them, while they gathered to erase
their personal histories —
as the next oncoming hoard gestated.

And I saw Cavafy[2] alone
awaiting their arrival to sew into his exile
a sky of barbarians,
and one great bird spreading out a tale
about its most recent chaos,
about the ancient sky,
about people who come down
to Mesopotamia (the land of blackness)
and collect their map of rains,
so the invaders can cleanse holiness
with the water of their killed people,
where dwarfs have a shadow, where trees
and flags are embroidered
with the vast hunger of my people.
What was the difference if they stayed,
these Pharos of the oasis,
or if they fell —
fertile solutions in the memory,
if they erected nations from oblivion
or if they dwelt in passing shadows?
What was the difference
if the invaders lost their way
to those who lived here before they arrived,
who hesitated before their arrival?
They were gathered and poisoned in nights of memories.

What if they had remained, wild against assault,
refusing to scatter
while the barbarians hovered at
the border, threatening!

I am among them.
The mirrors see what they see.
For what buffoon will the strait
be widened?
The great fire occurs
and Rome vanishes.
Its wreckage gleams in the dark anew:
freedom and barbarians.

[1] *Ur* was a city in ancient Sumer, located at the site of modern Tell el-Mukayyar in Iraq's Dhi Qar Governorate. Once a coastall city nearth the mouth of the then Euphrates River on the Persian Gulf, Ur is now well inland, south of the Euphrates on its right bank. *Anabasis* is the title of a seven-volume work by Xenophon about a long march of ten thousand Greek mercenaries to capture Persia (401 BC).

[2] Constantine P. Cavafy: (April 29, 1836-April 29, 1933) was a reknown Greek poet who lived in Alexandria and worked as a journalist and civil servant.

Translated by: Soheil Najm

Mohammed al-Nassar

Born in Nasiriah, 1961.
Published books:
The Current of the Days, Baghdad,
Competing Me on the Desert, Baghdad,
Third Life, Beirut, 1993.

Lies in an Inkpot

I needed clean ink
and fire to guard my waking,
to lead the defeated clouds,
with my stick—
passing by a rock snapped by rain,
torn cries,
and a decayed consolation,
calling at me: *O yesterday!*
How many cities does the pain need
to be just,
when it passes lakes of blood,
and the lies of the wind
blacken our faces?

And you sick serpent
O life;
you swim in our tears
seeking for a missed sin or injured hope
at the gates of hell,
our gates of discontent,
go with soft efficiency
toward our cold sleep
to sting it with your poisoned light
and dragging the prey,
move it away like an amputated finger
to a broken mountain,
to a labyrinth of tranquil rumination,
and when you tire,
O serpent,
disguise yourself again,

since every city made of sand and deception,
is a peaceful shrine for you,
so roam,
roam
and engrave a high statue,
for this dizziness.

Translated by: Soheil Najm

When Will I Awaken From This Life?

Talking led me to the graveyard.
Talking with my friend,
who was speechless,
led me to the graveyard.

I could not return the ring to her.
It jumped from my brother's finger
at a washhouse for the dead
where I saw my country raving.
The river — I saw it
as a black knife.

O friend!
O neighbor!
O desert!
I was obliterated by your
stony rain, my eyes effaced,
my flight, obsessed and desolate,
unable to reach my country,
unable to reach exile.

O speechless friend
across a fallen fence!

O

I found a pigeon
that neither cried nor wailed.

Around it were drawings
of children without limbs
and I remembered,
O friend!
the ring
that slipped
from my brother's finger
and fell into the water.

Can we then find,
O friend, O neighbor!
the ones who were lost
in the graveyard itself lost
beneath another graveyard
that was red?

What you say is wrong
my friend, my neighbor!

The moon didn't fall.
The limb of the space
was broken.

What you say is wrong.

This is not crazy,
it is the Street,
long and desolate.

What you say is wrong.

This is not an injured sun,
it is the only sun
of a forlorn house.

People have left it,
gone away.

O friend, O neighbor, O desert!
nothing remains but winter buried
under a heap of firewood
and I almost smell the odor of fresh dead
rise up with this sand storm,
that put out the lamp you left over there.

O

O neighbor!
O Friend!

This is the black house.
These are its ghost inhabitants
and those are the banners,
like bleeding snow.

And when
arrows clash
everywhere,
when
the emperor
prepares another feast
for our foggy country
I will remember
rolling my eyes
over the washhouse
and the lies that swallow war.

I will arrange
chess pawns
on the table,
desperate,
but not dead
because
I can
move my teeth
and with my fist I can catch
the beasts of the wind
opening the door with this hand,
which the bird and the bough mock,
and when
the nightmare brings me back

to the "execution field,"
I will jump fully terrified
and scratch at the chest
of the poor light.

O friend, O neighbor!
I will inspect your forlorn window
and your tree that gives us figs
at the end of summer,
and with the fullness of my despair,
I will breathe this strange fresh sleek air like a memory
empty from the sense of dawn
full of dumb desire,
and I will surrender to sleep
because I will be a morsel to the animal of hope no longer.

As for life,
O friend, O neighbor, O desert!
as for this excellent cage
for taming sparrows and children,
as for the burning tears
my country weaned me on,
I swim in a sanctuary of ash
and go on
like wind,
rain,
or idols
putting
my ear on the track of that railway
that goes to the graveyard,
because I can do only one thing
in these ravaged times:

Continue
to wait for a miracle
to return my ring of shock,
and my country, to me
so I can awaken from
this life.

Translated by: Soheil Najm

Munthir Abdul-Hur
Born in Basra, 1961.
Published books:
Necklace of Mistakes, Baghdad, 1992.
Exercise in Oblivion, Baghdad 1997.

I, Too, Love Butterflies

I, too, love butterflies
but…
for seven years
I have not seen one

○

I saw, in the mirror,
a man standing
on his head.

The moon draws a confession—
he celebrates,
asks and appears
to those infatuated by conquest—
and is a dud with his woman,
on good terms with his madness.

Maybe he will not come
at dawn with calamity and two wings,
nor will he carry an axe to bless his name
among the chorus
that curses him one by one
and choses him — in secret —as a savior,
but he thought it right to knock down
the doors of the dead
that visit him in his dreams
and loosen the fears of his days.

His skin is vivid because of his calling
and his blood is ready to roam the streets of exile.
He is the one who scratched his face
to ascertain the color.
He is the one who wandered alone among friends
while they watched butterflies
falling into fire…

〇

I … too…
love butterflies
but you are far away from my salt
and a stranger to my isolation
which tempts me — every night—
and laments my books
which became birds
that flew from my shelves
and came back to me as…
lottery cards
and unpleasant breakfasts.

Translated by: Dr. Sadek R. Mohammed

Muqdad Masaud

Born in Basra, 1955
Published book:
The Illuminating Sunset (poems), Baghdad 2008.

False Roofs

The north wind is a sponge.
It dried out the basins of the sky
but the roof of our house is rain.
Five days and a half shaggy day.
The books,
the pictures,
the letters,
the inkpot,
my wings,
my grandfather's bronze beard,
and my errors, bulky
with the advice of those unable to find light,
are in the rain too.

Logic of Feathers

When we talk in darkness
why do they imagine that
we are talking about darkness?
The bird has two wings.
There are feathers in the wings,
When they talk about feathers
why do we imagine them talking about the bird?

I have a step, a sparrow high,
in the south of remembrance,
taking me to the north of tomorrow.

Translated by: Soheil Najm

Mustafah Abdulah

Born in Basra 19__ and died in Morocco 1990.
Published book:
The Beautiful Foreigner, Baghdad 2004.

The Horse

O, yesterday
be kindhearted. The horse
submitted to having his neck broken.
The sun was
hitting the mud…
and the eye
with the sand in the mud,
and the eye
with the sand on the tongue—

O

In the past
the earth was endless
under the leg of the horse.
The wind could not come upon
the neighing of the horse.
The shadow of the horse on the sand
was a roof for the people there—

O

O, yesterday
be kindhearted, the glass was broken:
Who bent down
to collect the horse…?

Translated by: Soheil Najm

The Beautiful Foreigner

I am the beautiful foreigner.
I am the foreigner and this is my tongue
that desires
and doesn't feel shy
so it grows longer!

I am the foreigner confused between my shirt
and this light darkness.
You appear to me out of him yet you never
find me with him.
I am confused between my shirt and my weak skin.
You appear to me out of him bewitched
by the sound of the masks.

O

I am the foreigner tripled by attendants and rising
to the dining table on one foot,
the clean speech started
and the dishes washed.
I'd hoped to protest but
remembered that I came without my mouth
and I left my long tongue
with the ink…in my pen.
I'm the foreigner I hoped to protest
but I didn't find the speech.
I remembered my voice bid farewell to me.
How then could I say
and sit up
        on my seat while it was staggering among chairs?

I am the foreigner
I tripled the power of until I was unmasked. The focus narrowed,
        they were using me for the candles,
        the perfume and the slips
        in the inspiration of the cigarettes.

I hear it
        and the expiration of the smoke
        so I wipe my face with my sleeve
        and I come close to the dinning table.

O, where could I hide the card to hide my name?
Where could I change this shirt speckled by date palms?
I imagined that I was naked among knives.
Like her the faces faced me with their surnames
naked at the exit.

O

I am the foreigner who closed the book.
I entered the luggage waiting for the train.
I'm the foreigner.
My surname is with me
and I am not alone but, in essence, alone.

O

I am the foreigner
I knew my limits.
I invented a paper country for my country.
— It is a packet of cigarettes —
And when anxious ones appeared in cafés
following me like a matchstick,
I collected my luggage, lit my cigarette,
then I went away,
light,
burning…!

○

I am the beautiful foreigner.
I stood with those who stood,
I thronged, but I was in a small place.
I deviated
to let the luggage cross before me
to let the place cross before me
and time to cross before me.
I learned to wait
and make a country for myself in a passport.

Translated by: Soheil Najm

Muwafak Mohamed

Born in Hilla, 1947
Published books:
Hilli Flirtation, Zurich-Bahdad, 2007,
Abdeel, Baghdad, 2007.

Fatwas For Rent

Whoever, among you, sees an Iraqi,
should slaughter him with your hand, but if you
can't, then with a mortar canon, and if you can't,
then with a car bomb and this is the least of Faith.
Narrated by Qaradhawi[1] while he was drinking the blood of Iraqis
and relishing their livers with ecstasy since, as he claims,
this is palatable to the drinkers.
Our people bleed and you gnaw livers —
an Iraqi and spiteful?
And we endure!
because God created Iraqis from Job's clay
after mingling it with Adam's cognizance
and Abraham's patience.
This is a time, wherein the slightest thing is a blade
engaged to the throat. Good work!
Will you continue digging your slaughtered grave in the poem
and say, *No,*
to those who sell homeland
as your bloodied hands approach an eye that will spark
in its grave-clothes?
Stir up the eye with your hands,
leave your whiteness near its teardrop to finish the poem
and take this iron and make it broth!
The starving people are agonized.
Don't forget!
Cook that agony on a low fire made of their flesh
so that it becomes ready at the end of the century.
Serve the meal fresh to their grandchildren!
And we endure!
The land is our land, now, while
we know that the slaughtering fatwas
recommend the slaughterer's heart, if he has one.

Have no mercy upon the slaughtered
and therein, the toughest…
nothing is tougher than hell.
I'm fire, why should I fear sparks?
Its ringing sigh is still ringing in our ears and eyes
as we sweep our sons' flesh in the streets.
One heap here, another there.
And blood is seen
conversing with its holder and flying to heaven.
Seest thou not the sky is blood red in Iraq,
and the wind is crying out, weeping, from our mothers' chests,
hiding its whimper in the wings of doves that fly not?
And the Tigris and the Euphrates are two gaping wounds
jam packed with slaughtered corpses
and floods are storming high mountains,
but we built not the arch?
We say not to the earth: "O mother carry us faithfully!"
We are dashing to plunder or surrender.
Iraq is luggage tucked and lost in lands of exile,
and what is left
or
who is left
becomes the third firedog.
And we endure!
The bleeding is from us
and the slaughterers and indoctrinators of fatwas
are going to hell.
But if any of you is ill, or on a journey,
then murder ten Iraqis.
And when you can not find a sword, then betake yourself a good ax,
and give glad tidings to satellite channels.
Who, among you, is a Sayyed?[2]
An old man said: "Me."
And they dragged him and slaughtered him
and performed ritual ablution with his blood
and prayed afternoon prayer.
And the swordsman, who causes the sword to enter into the throat
and causes the throat to enter into the sword, recited,
and he hath power over all slaughters:
"I pray, yet, know not, when I slaughter him,

is it two I prayed for this afternoon, or eight?"
O ye slaughterers!
Your mothers' wombs slip away, bleeding, from their tombs
seeking refuge in Allah from Satan the outcast
and inquiring about who was congealed in them;
was he created from a gushing fluid?
Or was he a devil that came to her the moment Iraq
was opened up to hell?
"We slaughtered them not, they slaughtered themselves,"
said a mufti from happy Yemen
We had lived in their graveyards during the days of Hubal[3]
as he was chewing Qat[4] in a nap in which he was turning
his testicles about to the right and to the left.
But there is no supporter
to call for a crooked Yemeni daggers donation campaign,
to present them, sparkling, to the veiled men
with the promise of paradise
and plentiful Iraqi blood casks to intoxicate the non-believer
before the believer.
And we endure.
Iraq is our Iraq.
May Allah, because of it, disgrace cross-border slaughterers!
We pray in hell
and support each other,
have we, then, no intercessors to intercede on our behalf?
Isn't there a man in this nation that seeks murder
from the cradle to the grave
and issues fatwas contrary to the will of its Prophets?
Isn't there a Salih[5] in the people of Thamud[6]
shouting, "The heads of Iraqis are on spears;
Allah and His messengers are free from liability to the veiled men!"
The Iraqi blood that you shed
is what is left of the blood of the Prophets, Ali[7] and Hussein!
A wound as long as fifteen centuries is still bleeding and bleeding
and your spades are still plowing it!
Does power have all this charm?
Has the murderer and architect of mass graves,
digging grooves two meters deep and half a meter wide so that
a slaughtered person can't kick,
become a mujahid while he is killing what's left of Iraqis?

Where were you when Iraq was a machine mincing human flesh?
Weren't we Arabs and Muslim then?
Haven't you heard that the abundance of skulls and bones
was as high as the sky?
And the sky cracked and showered us with graves?
Isn't it time for this nation's thinkers and masters
to put the sword they laid on our necks aside?
And we endure.
Iraq is the father of all crises. Since the creation of everything
it has enjoyed not its two rivers.
It felt not safe of fear.
It fed not its starving people
but it is a country and a root.
And we endure.
And continue to bandage the wounds of Iraq
and support its sons.
This bleeding boy will rise and show mercy on his murderers
and reunite his palm trees
and carry the Tigris in a procession to the Euphrates.
Fertility is certainly coming.
This is our last chance.
Our brooklets are filling their breasts with honey
to silence the cries of our suckling fields.
O my land! God be with you as you fight in the depth of the sea
of monsters and cross the flood of blood!
Heaven trembles when it beholds the remains of your children,
dusts off its moon and stars
and stretches out its hand to your forehead to shine upon it
and show the world
that Iraq is alive and will never die.

1. Qaradhawi (born 1926) is a radical Egyptian cleric.
2. Sayyed is a descendent of the Prophet Mohammed family.
3. *Hubal* was a god worshiped by Arabs before Ismal.
4. *Qat* refers to the Catha edulius shrub. Its fresh young leaves are chewed as a stimulant in Yemen;
5. *Salih* was a prophet in the Holy Quran;
6. *Thamud* were a people in north Arabia. The prophet Salih was sent to them;
7. *Ali* refers to Imam Ali, Prophet Mohammed's cousin and the rightful successor to him accordig to Shia Islam.

Translated by: Dr. Sadek R. Mohamed

Nasif al-Nasiry

Born in Baghdad, 1962.
Published book:
In the Light of the Spike That Is Prepared to Sacrifice,
Zurich-Baghdad, 2007.

Nature Is Our Heritage

Nature is our heritage, in contrast to history,
a settled mythology shaking dust from mathematics,
blowing fire in the heavy eyelashes of stars,
in the code of days,
in a feverish momentum starting from music.
It is a renewal of knowledge about gold that steals journeys
and fighting lines which turn and maneuver from old wars.
Nature sleeps with its husband, death, in all seasons
and renews the kinship between animal and rain,
between a piece of wood and a thunderbolt,
between a mutinously clean rose and the hawk's claw,
a discontinuous melody, no language made it,
but a fountain of death, sharp rocks and the moss hobbled to them.
Nature whets its gloomy self and shreds our dreams
that hang in the corridors of our lamps.
Death.

Translated by: Soheil Najm

Nature's Lesson

The fire coal of annihilation is flaring up this summer
night that is dangling without silver.
Creatures are decaying and taking gelatinous shapes.
Our lips are wet with the rain of insomnia
and shivering without any hope in the desert of the world.
Snows of mirage extinguish the lamps of our hopes.
What is the whole value of our perishing lives?
The hours given to us are but drops in the oceans of time.
We open the gate of eternity. The dark shadow of our existence
is dragging us and we ask, "Does death destroy life or existence?"
O, nature: You who liberate us from love, pain, birth and death—
Is nature really this crystal human being full of beauty and sanctuary
whenever he ascends toward the abyss, these tigers that assist
the thunderbolt, the blessed birds that are raining over the trees,
the fish, the seeds, the butterflies which are breathing the pasture'9s air,
the jungle, the agitated insects in their wild languages, the voices
and the perfumes hanging on our necks, all of them will disappear after
a very short time letting death take care of them with its venerable snow?
The barren edges.
The decaying.

Translated by: Soheil Najm

The Matter, the Senses, the Idea and the Atoms

In stone, rivers, grass, space, mountains,
planets, in the eye of the animal, the temples, the feathers of time,
the outstretched hand of the spike and the breath
of the bough under the snow,
there is neither existence for the soul nor for the mind.
How could the soul reach to liberate from matter
the burning bramble beyond the creation?
Is there joy in endlessness
or are dust and nature the trick?
In our longing and thirst for the invisible, we invent gods
for their symbolic content to understand eternal springs.
Death in death
and love in death.
Atoms are spinning,
oscillations are reacting.
The blue agate of the soul is flaring in the essence
of our eternal torture.
Our gods are images and myths.
Jesus doesn't accept the Hindu transmigration
and Buddha is refusing the Christian trinity.
Does the world have any purpose?
Does it have any cause or meaning?
In this slim flower that is shivering in the summer night
there is petal, corolla, trunk, sap,
pistil and leaves.
Beauty alone is the lamp of the soul,
it shines and rains from the sky of the material world
which embraces eternity.

Translated by: Soheil Najm

Ra'ad Abdulqadir

Born 1950, died in 2003.
Published books:
Let the Nightingale Wonder, Baghdad, 1996,
A Hawk, a Sun Over His Head: Baghdad, 2002.

Let the Nightingale Wonder

Let the nightingale
wonder
at the hand of disaster
that trains him as a falcon.

O

Let freedom
remember its form;
let the world
test its wit.
It is just a bird,
unimportant
entirely
whether it sings of the disaster
or swoops down on the prey

O

Let the nightingale
wonder.

Translated by: Soheil Najm

Windows

They can do everything,
look inside or outside,
they can notice any movement in the air.
In place, they don't care about what happens.
They are silent, gazing, convinced,
happy with their love stories,
with light penetrating their bodies.
They enjoy their loneliness,
aloft…
windows.

15th of Oct. 2001

Translated by: Soheil Najm

Ra'ad Mutashar

Born in Baghdad, 1963.
Published books:
The Drowned Are Collecting Coral, Baghdad 1996,
I Am Dripping From My Wrist, Tunisia 2003.

Kirkuk

O, grave walking in a gulf; regret is filling me.
The city, a beginning that is filled with flying newspapers;
the city, a child filled with questions runs after a truck;
he cuts pearls of light with his intoxicated laugh;
the city, an old man on the bridge crossing to your lonely castle;
the city, a vast hut…so from your chimneys time begins
flourishing in the faces, in my mother's incense
on Thursday evenings and in the awaking of legends.
O, garden of exodus to the exile of unknown
did I oppress you, city of fable, mother of retreating mistakes,
north of south… and south of the heart that is surrounded
with secrets? For you the brook of the north is wandering
in its veiled maze behind the history of mirrors,
and under the pearl of your mole, the doves shelter continually
braiding the flower of eternal flame.
So have you seen the flame's braids in a cold hour
smashing misfortune's owl, crowning the woman of gold
with spells on the bed of queens who stink
like gloomy clothes?
O, torch that is hung on a cloud, I'm coming to you.
Take my eyes to cut the pain, take my shoulders bearing the horizon,
take my hands writing the first letter of your name,
take whatever you wish.
Order me and I'll be your poet, your history allocated among wishes,
your window trapped with birds, your balance wrecked from
generations falling on the grass, your waters that drink
from the fish of spells and from the navel of a horizon
fogged with pastures. You take whatever you wish.
O, deer of dream surrounded by the symbol,
how come you attached to pain a bed of clouds?!
O, mouth of birth, like a necklace around your suburbs,

our suburbs which are open to grain, water and lightning.
O, poetry of my days, the food of my perfume,
and the descendant of my sand, from you, for you, I begin
and finish the road of my running.
On your earth the feet of the poor are extinguished.
In you and from you, I touch the symbol of myself.
In your yesterday, in my yesterday,
and from the fatigue of the people, I collect beads of sun
under the arbors of particle rain from your domes.
To be a country lulls me under a poor star.
So have you been born under misfortune's vanishing star?!
Tell me: "Do you come from the feathers of imagination?
Or you were a harp of clouds lowered on farms?!"
I'm kissing in you trees of moderation, I walk with your boat
in pastures of prophesies dangling from poor clothes
and their melting torch. Who greeted you? Peace,
city of castles dangling from horizon's keys.
They circled you with hymns and happiness
and they grew stars in your gardens that bore fruit,
your castle painted ... like the question.

O my city of whiteness
    let me sing my
        favorite song,
          How many times.
            I laughed, cried, shuddered, throbbed
              like the gulf of optimism
              calling
               I
                love you
                 Kirkuk.

Kirkuk-Baghdad, 6/12/1994

Translated by: Soheil Najm

Ra'ad Zamil

Born in 1970 in Imarah (South of Iraq).
Published one book of poetry in 2009 in Baghdad.

A Practice in Distraction

1
No train waits for me
nor station.
I am just a passerby
holding my age
          as if it were a bag of trash.
    I stand at a crossroads
where all roads
lead to distraction.

All over the world
the seed can
be a tree
and the tree can be a forest,
only in this land
the forest retreats to be a tree,
the tree becomes a seed,
the seed after that
becomes a disgrace
on the forehead
of a wasteland.

For the emperor
who took my blood
as fuel in the wars,
for the father
who made
my back
like a camel in the desert,
for the woman
who disappointed me
at the beginning of the age

and for the friends
who wove my existence
on the poetry table
            without memory,
all of them
must correct my life
I will not chase them,
convincing only with hooting
like an owl,
to witness this destruction.

2
Every thing vanishes
in the ruins
which we call the houses,
every thing vanishes.
Only misery
gleams like a scandal
and in the bitter darkness
whenever I see
a spider on the roofs
I invite it to the meal of loneliness
to be my drinking companion
in this distraction.

Translated by: Soheil Najm

Reem Qais Kubba

Born in Baghdad, 1967.
Published books:
Seagulls Committing Flying, Baghdad, 1991,
Celebrating Waste Time, Baghdad, 1999,
I Close My Wings and Steal Time For Writing, Cairo, 1999.

Heeltap

The wine is from your eyes,
from my eyes the milk of the breast
kindled with longing.
From my hands abundance of wings,
from your hands pin strings, hot needles
penetrating feathers
dispersing love spray —
lips or a waist
or a leg, kicking at the limits of
what can be said
in this appointed time.

We don't take…we give
we don't grant…we are plundered,
and I stretch out on the fluff of the earth
as particle of dust
announcing the hunger of cities,
ships, songs and afflictions.

O

Eagerly I drink your eyes,
as a child licks their mother's milk drops.

O

…and I wake up:
       your female is shackled
          and my boy is without lips.

Baghdad 14th of Oct. 1995

An Earring

My single earring is with you.

O

Usurers will come after awhile
and evening will end the wailing of the foreheads
while my killers take me
                        with them.

O

Still my single earring
            is with you.

Hilla 25th of May 1989

Heeltap and *An Earring*, Translated by: Soheil Najm

Apples

You are gone
and hide my morning in your hands.

○

You'll come a little after the dryness
of the lips.

Do you mind if I keep your apple with me?
Bite it when longing wrangles with me
                              to stay fresh
and you will come back to find me brimful…
                    in my apple fullness?!

Baghdad 12th of August 1996

Translated by: Soheil Najm

A Kiss

It was neither lips
           nor a touch
                      nor even a sip from honey saliva.

○

It was a perfume
        for a whisper of transparent honesty
                sublime
                   showering me with kisses.

Baghdad, 12th of August1996

Translated by: Soheil Najm

A Shirt

What
if I enter
under your shirt
sitting
at the left corner
to take a breath from you
and plant
a poem
between your ribs?

Baghdad 2nd of Nov. 1995

Translated by: Soheil Najm

A Stick

Do not hold a stick in the middle
as you wrap your arms around my waist
since your stick is not a female
and I'm not a piece of wood.

Baghdad 1st of Nov.1995

Translated by: Soheil Najm

A Rose

What
if my palm
   were a rose?
      You would pick it up
        and kiss it.

You would smell my fragrance
without fear.
....
  But,
 O dear,
   I would wither
      from passion.

2nd of April 1998

Translated by: Soheil Najm

Sa'ad Jasim

Born In Babel, 1960.
Published Book:
Spaces of the Speech Child, Baghdad, 1990.

This Is the Question

O mother
you are my father's plowed field,
the bed of his primitive desire,
and the house of his offspring
where death spared only me.
Why have you left the angels,
the angels of white prayers,
taken me out of
your vast paradise
to a world more narrow
than the eye of a mouse?

Mother…Ah!…
Why have you let them take me out,
expelled,
like my old father?

Translated by: Dr. Sadek R. Mohammed

Singularity

Creatures of this time have goals
and ways.
But I,
the one who is heavily armed with fears,
misgivings,
and worries,
have never
chosen a goal
and do not intend to make peace with other's ways
because I have
my ways, which
all the earth cannot border,
never!...... not even this horizon.

Translated by: Dr. Sadek R. Mohammed

Safa Thiyab
Born in Nasiria 1970.
Published books:
Anxious, Baghdad 2001.
No One But Me, Baghdad 2005.

A Green Rock

Insanity
will come always where you never come.

Insanity
is this split cloud from which falls what was never water.

Insanity too
is empty streets… and a broom scowling before dust.

And this thing that splits every day is insane too.

He bows in his uniform that looks like a garden.
His mind does not look like any rock.

Translated by: Sadek R. Mohammed

Who Knows?

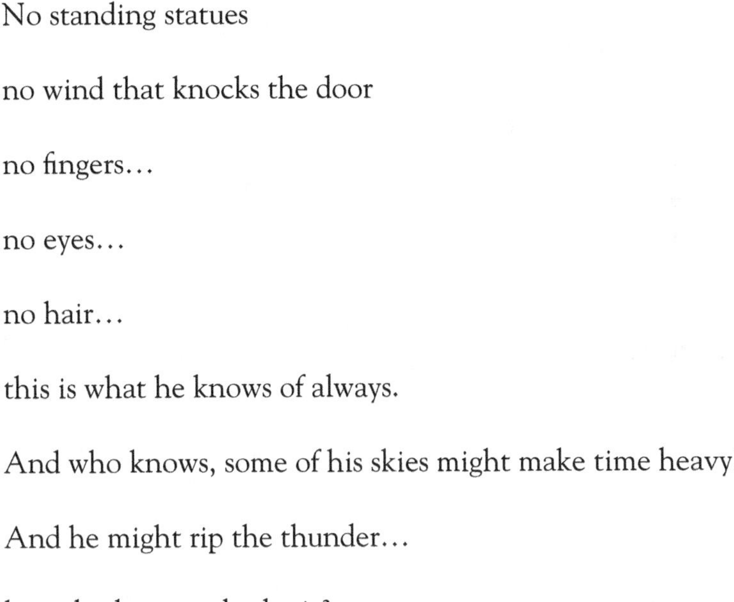

No standing statues

no wind that knocks the door

no fingers…

no eyes…

no hair…

this is what he knows of always.

And who knows, some of his skies might make time heavy?

And he might rip the thunder…

but who knows who he is?

Translated by: Dr. Sadek R. Mohammed

The Iraqi

Every time he sees the blooming of a flower,
the sun blazes him, so he escapes indoors.

Every time the day is about to set,
darkness attacks him,
so he loses the garden.

Translated by: Dr. Sadek R. Mohammed

A God

The sky that split

was nothing but my lips.

The land that was enraged

was nothing but my eyes.

And the mountains that were leveled

were nothing but my fingers…

O

And I am a god

pushing you into the abyss.

Translated by: Dr. Sadek R. Mohammed

Salah Hassan
Born in Babel
Published books:
I Go Out With Broken Compass, Lehigh, 1997,
The Deleted, Beirut.

Postponed Geography

Come forward female
soul of the forest…
Your wet body
with its smells and tenderness
awakens in my blood
a crowd of questions,
calls me to set traps
awakes feeling in my arms.
Come forward female.
Your body with its arcs and bending
awakens in my imagination
primitive fathers,
predators
ready to swoop down,
wild fathers
hunting storms,
make a scarf from them
for their prey.
Come forward female,
your body
with its fruits
that wild suns
and the light of remote stars
have ripened
is awakening in my memory
a totem.
I should dance around it every day
in order not to die…
Come forward female,

O glee of good health,
how could this geography
be sad
when your body is
a boat upon it?!

Translated by: Soheil Najm

The Statue of the Poet

It's I
who watched the angels
and saw them dancing
around my statue.
I saw pigeons
peck at the pocket of my shirt
and build a nest near my heart.
I heard the madmen saying,
"The poet is the creature who runs away
to his certainty,"
and they add:
"Craziness is an incomplete leap to the impossible."
I saw widows
search my face
for a man who went to war
and never returned.
I saw men looking into
the dust for a star they wasted.
I saw them
circling me without wings or singing.
I saw photographers
with their cameras that make
this place sleepless
looking for the sadness
in my laugh.
It's I
who at the end of the night
watch drunkards
and see them urinating on my statue.

Translated by: Soheil Najm

Reception Party

Perplexed, in period costume
like a Shakespearean character,
my death is chasing me.
In spite of his tough appearance
and care for details
his steps, for a mysterious reason,
seem worried.
Maybe because of his new shoes.
It hurts to see him perplexed
like this.
To let him relax
I'll invite him tonight
to have drink with me.
I'll close my eyes
so that he can put poison
in my cup.
I may pretend while
going to the bath that
I don't want to see
his quivering hand —
so he can do his job.
My life has failed
I don't want my death
to fail.

Translated by: Soheil Najm

Run Away From the Family

It wasn't a bad idea
when I dreamt of having a house
and living in it.
It wasn't a bad idea
when I dreamt of finding a woman
and marrying her.
It wasn't a bad idea
when I drew four kids
and they were born.
Nor was it a bad idea
when I drew a back door
for the house
and fled.

Translated by: Soheil Najm

Salam Dawai

Born In Baghdad, 1970.
Published Book:
That Bitter Rain, Baghdad, 1998

My Country

How could I leave you
without falling down
like a fugitive letter?
How could I say farewell to you,
O my aged pain,
O my pierced lung?
You are the wind
and I am the mouth, the bleeding voice
and the afflicted eyes.

O

O tremors of wide-eyed hope
like the eyes of martyrs
diminished like remote gloss…
O whispers of lovers
that are concealed
by poverty…
O poverty that is floating over gold…
O yells of poor vendor boys,
and their vendor fathers…
O mothers of tears
and hot invocations
ascending to God in flame…
O God's road toward poverty…
O the pauper's road to black bread
and arid dream…
O most delicious black bread…
O most glorious arid dream…
O deeper than pure sadness…
O more yellow than assassinated joy…
O whiter than an impious promise…

O more embarrassed than a pending dream…
O deeper than a deep wound…

How could I leave
and what could I say to these minarets?
What could I say to visitors sending their pain
to holy men behind the windows,
to the windows?
The windows have eyes.
O my country,
O my cage,
oh, my forever exile…!
O my death that lifts my hand
to God...

Translated by: Soheil Najm

In My Head

Thick clouds travel in my head.
A mistake buzzes... falls
and buzzes.
I tempt it as an idea,
I kiss it like a friend
and ... do I gnaw it as a piece of bread?
I do not, like a prophet, say,
"Not only on bread can man live."
I am not jobless by inheritance
to clap, smile foolishly.
I am jobless by poetry,
or a poet by disaster
so I can tell myself
"O, self, resort to the mistake,
give form to the mistake itself,"
only can poets live on mistakes.
And I tell my beloved,
"I am a heart that pulses aimlessly,
so forget me like an annoying obsession
and sleep, O my beloved, calmly."
And I say to my friends,
"Go far away so that I cannot aggravate you
because I am excessive, like a disease."
And I tell my teacher,
"I am your prominent mistake,
like a big nose
I am your problem."
Yet I have no problem
just thick clouds
traveling in my head.

Translated by: Soheil Najm

Poems

1
Dangling from my feet
amidst an infinite vacuum,
if I fall,
I fall in nothingness
and if I ascend —
I never can—
can any one ascend — in reverse?

2
When he exploded
nobody fell,
nobody fled,
nobody cared.
So he collected his fragments
and disappeared, ashamed.

3
The wounds
became enchanted trees.
Whenever the wind shook its boughs
unbelievable fruits fell down.

4
Because the front was a circle
we vacated the barricades
and took refuge death
by death.

5
Since you are a bad myth
written by the bones of the centuries
that groan in the abyss of time,
you'll never be beautiful, O my life!

Translated by: Soheil Najm

Salman Dawood Mohammed

Born In Baghdad, 1956.
Published Book:
My Distinguished Mark, Baghdad, 1996.

Unarmed Morning

From whence shall I get a falcon to rule
the grandeur of the road
or a hand to harvest the rabbits
from the garden of the skull?
Even lakes that brandish an early decency
imagine flight at noon.
I wonder if time wears a shirt dabbled
with dusk intentionally
fallen from an autumn of pedestals,
or do we pile up, cold, like a fallen soldier
in an ebony box?
Trachoma settles in the heart
erasing connectivity with diaspora
and we trot between the whip and the reward,
toward a bastard splendor.
I wonder who would save the wailing of the fingers
from the curse of the cocoon.
I wonder
who would
beckon…?

Translated by: Dr. Sadek R. Mohammed

Shaker Laibi
Born in Baghdad, 1955.
Published Books:
Fingers of Stone, Baghdad, 1976,
The Text of the Three Texts, Beirut, 1982,
Calls For Help, Damascus, 1984,
Eloquence: A Text and Twenty Sketches, Geneva 1988,
Metaphysic, Geneva, 1996,
How, Beirut, 1997

The Unshod Ladies Went on Foot

The unshod ladies went on foot
to visit gold —
completely naked except for the clank of the anklet
and the scent of henna.
Their mood was like an open window
and their hearts were captive
to the sound of cicadas hidden in heavy clouds.
The flower was naked too
except for its scent roaming in the air.
The unshod ladies amassed
in one mirror
that was smashed suddenly
and the sparrow, the female of the sparrow, the sparrow
stood nearby singing of the wreckage.

Geneva 24/12/2001

Translated by: Dr. Sadek R. Mohemmed

Scorpions Are Relaxing in the Darkness of the Garden

Scorpions are relaxing in the darkness of the garden;
a little light will upset them.
Such is the truth
a little logic
will cause its dimensions to bulge.
The scent of the dust they breathe
grows old under their feet
as myths grow old
between your tender fingers
as they stretch in the thickness of my hair.
Your fingers are frittering on my back
as if they were five lizards petrified
eternally.
Are you still wet and waiting
at the doorstep?

Geneva 23-12-2001

Translated by: Dr. Sadek R. Mohammed

Shawqi Abdulamir
Born in Nasiria, 1949.
Published books:
A Speech For the Arabia Singer, 1976,
Borders, 1980,
Ababeel, 19850,
The Seven Inscriptions, 1992.

Yesterday I Met a Country

Yesterday I met a country, a street connecting death to the sea,
language for a celestial post, the stone remembered and the sparrows
were brighter than a bullet in the sky.
In the first evening,
the sea was small and covered by night white doves,
fond of drizzle and pellets.
Beirut was red islands and the dictionary of blood.
Another evening
Beirut burned again in the corpse of Jeanne d'Arc
rising from the coffin of victory.
The third evening?
Time was a wail hiding behind the sea.
The fourth evening,
faces were a panel on the pavement
of those killed in a revolution.
The fifth evening
Beirut was the angry woman of the East.
The sixth evening
the bullet was the female of the age.
The seventh evening
was a night in a tomb.

O

The burnt sea forgot the water's ash.
The bird forgot the phoenix wings.
Beirut forgot the remains of the corpse in its midst.
The wall forgot the faces of the martyrs.

The street forgot all our windows penetrated
by poetry and news.
Time forgot a path opened between revolution and strangers.
History forgot the enemy's cemeteries.
The face forgot the face
and things forgot things.

O

Between the step and the step
I forget that I am dangling,
I fire up a window
and smoke.

O

Yesterday I met a country. I entered it through all boundaries
and crossed all boundaries for it. I came to a runaway tree
alive in "Alfakhani"[1] and collected a meeting in "Alrusafah"[2].
Does this home shelter me in medals for death?
Tonight, I fell from cities of poetry to an earth of words
and tore my cry of gloomy silence.
I open in my death
a window for death.

O

Yesterday I met a country
and I left it
looking for a country.

[1] Alfakhani: A district in Beirut.
[2] Alrusafah: The east side of Baghdad.

Translated by: Soheil Najm

A Stone on This Weeping

You began with me falling loftily
like a dying bird
and then you left a lump of years
bloodstained from a silent call.
Yet I am neither the way to you
nor the sign in the way.
If a cloud was awakened at the right time
it wouldn't necessarily bear water
nor promise lightning.
I'll come to you from pale trees,
from impossible steps,
from blood in the messages,
from a weeping stone
and from a bullet fenced by hand.
O quarrel.
I give it sophisticated words
and waiting
cut my feet on it.

Translated by: Soheil Najm

A Third Bank

(Excerpt)

Who is going to extinguish silence in the stone
and the walls of joy in the rose?
Who is going to steal from the window of cloudlessness
the secrets of awakening?
Who is going to break this horizon
in the wing of a bird?

O

When tears become sap
your history will be wood.
Neither the wave
nor the grass,
nor our drowned people
know this river that stands in me without banks.

Translated by: Soheil Najm

Siham Jabbar
Born in Baghdad.
Published book:
The Poetess, Baghdad 1995.

Texts

1
Oblivion returned to me.
I am pregnant again
with its daughter, memory.

2
The sky had fallen,
our heads sharpened it!

3
A woman stays in the air.
No windows fly from her eyes

4
No lover is hiding in the jam.
Only a star gleams in its temperament.

5
This dancer remembers
the happiness of the fallen worlds.

The woman is a man and a little more.
She remains less than zero
to liberate herself from excess!

6
Run and die
then run and be the fire of that marathon.

7
Jump, this is a big valley,
called your age!

8
They became widowers
and their women were widows too!

9
The woman is patient,
the burden is thirst.
Who could pluck distance from the road?

10
They took the seesaw
and left me in the air.

Translated by: Soheil Najm

Like Hypatia[1] in Ancient Times

My hands are but your hands
and your mouth is one of my lips.
You are some of my darkness,
yet only darkness is needed to complete
the lonely woman's throne.
Still,
you are neither my finger,
nor are you my hands,
you are neither the confused eyes in the darkness,
nor are you the darkness
and there is no throne for a lonely woman.

Like Hypatia in ancient times
they skinned my body
as I counted the mathematical
relationship
of time eternal
on our bodies.
And as I patched that skin,
I squeezed witness from their eyes
and found they were not as they seemed
but I was still as I was.
I took a bath by all those philosophies,
by the beheaded sculptures,
while I was surrounding the killers
by a wall.
They could be the Barbarians,
they could be the Bedouins in their straying.
The gods sentenced
the labyrinth to grow among our fingers
since every hand is lost
and every love is wilderness.
What could the monsters see
in my blood?
A hand will pass through my heart,
squeeze the passion from it,
and they will take me in a coffin.

The coffin is a weapon then
and death is a new explosion that
smears the labyrinth with blood.
We sentenced more than these
decades on you.
The thirties had passed
but the forties had not,
the century had not.
Survival is for the fittest
and I'm not the fittest.
They are allocating my blood.
My arteries are for a wise man's death,
my brain is the food of Satan.
Still they get drunk.
Yet you are still heedless,
inject your blood with silence,
inject your love with patience.
Why do you hatch children?
Fast.
Every time the decades pass
you break away more.
Yet the mathematical relationship
won't be complete unless pupils keep
this wisdom in vials.
How much did the thorn flourish while you stayed
in the vial, you who are in full bloom!
These drops leap
so not to be a rose perfume.
How much did a spring vanish and a country begin
dancing in the cradle, never sleeping,
cutting the placenta and never being born?
Go away, O country
leave your dust, your sky,
your oil,
leave my dress,
leave it and get up
as if you were a runaway people,

as if I were giving birth to you and forgot,
as if you were an impious son
I prevented from inheritance.
I am just a lonely woman
and you are only…that traitor again.

22/5/2005

1. Hypatia was a Platonic philosopher and mathematician who was born and died in Alexandria in Egypt. One of the sacrifices of science in history, she was beheaded and skinned because of her liberal thinking.

Translated by: Soheil Najm

Soheil Najm

Born in Baghdad, 1956.
Published books:
Breaking the Phrase, Beirut, 1994,
I Am Your Carpenter Oh Light, Damascus, 2002,
No Paradise Outside the Window, Baghdad, 2008.

A Sparrow Rubbed By the Flute

1
It comes to me
that I may see what is invisible
in the pleasure of speech,
in a night walk
in the crawling of roses on myrtle.

It comes to me
that I may traverse the sea of experience,
embrace the sea of language,
since the world transforms obsession
into a song and its secrets into color.
This is my soul approaching
a stranger's fantasies,
casting afar to an abstract place,
rushing ahead to tame time,
passing with no hope for rescue
from the kings of drowning.

It comes to me
that I prefer resistance to leaving,
a mistake exaggerated and gleaming,
and accept this walk
through stagnant water.

2
I may not do well in the art of living
and I may stumble past light,
because love is a mutable speck, dust,
and I have nothing but the invisible guarding me.

To expel my whims
I structure myself
on the extension of a flower.
I stretch out my arm
to plant happiness
on the pores of meaning.
"Hey, meaning,
what if the victorious ones sat
in an open pocket?"
I am qualified to advise you—
you who live
in the navel of ink,
to single out a ray for death—
I may advise oblivion
not to escape
lest wind strip it
or waiting snip its
shadow.
Visions emerge
from me
and never come back.
Colors emerge too,
drinking their fog,
rising from me
surfaces excite wide flower beds.

3
These are my blue voices
and my gardens wet with intimacy.
These are my rains
and my horse
that is kneeling down
over the noise.
This is my time,
time of azure skies
and speeding orbits.
As if
I wanted what he didn't want—
I wanted my wing and my shadow.

I wanted the map of the lost soul.
I wanted my broken life.
I wanted to sing
the eyes of the stars embracing me.
I wanted to propagate wishes
and to set free language
I wanted…
tomorrow in a morning like this.

Translated by the poet

The Song of Wandering Basra

Between wake and sleep
I open my heart, hers is like a door
and I knock.
She shouts, "Who are you?"
People are asleep
but my woman awakes from fear,
barefoot at the sea, she
covers the sands with her heart,
wraps herself with the instant
and water.
"Hey...
Who are you?"
Hoarsely I call back.
My memory falls away
at the "Breiha"[1] roads.
She says,
"O vague, remote man!"

Here it is again, the closed door.
Should I knock?
In a bell tumult below al-Ashar[2] River
my soul splinters.
In front of the Indian market [3]
it will resurrect.
Our beloved will desert us today
to her boat across the river…
What do you want?
No heart is here to beat for you,
no stones to reverberate your night echo
and the river is strange.
It hurries at night to shelter
and al-Korah[4] is woven
from waves of war and sorrow —
the remains of a child lying
in the river bed.

What do you want?
Neither the beloved cares
nor the sea,
nor a ghost of guards at Bab-Zubair[5].
I drown in al-Kandaq[6]
and smell love as ash.
I drink the voices of our pleasures
when they are date palms
dancing when the jinn surprises them.
What do you want?
Troops of sharks snap at my heart.

The door doesn't open.
The Shanasheel of Basra are broken with tears.
I shout, longing barks in my bosom,
waiting for the latch.
I look up and darkness sets in.
Windows of the city disappear in clouds.
My steps are diverted to date palms
which illusion plants along my path.
I call out, "O, if rivers could sleep
on a wish or a drop of light…"

Who is this wanderer?
A monster lies deep within me,
"O, be closed my doors…"
But …I sing for her innocence and shout,
"O, my beloved,
Why do you deny me this night?"
My glow fades as I knock at your door.
Why should I sail
when the wind fills me with rage,
when my beloved flees her home?

"O, my beloved..."
I'm still shouting, shouting
my heart overburdened with a dream
knocking at your door
between wake and sleep.

13th of Feb 1994

Poet's note: 1, 2, 3 and 5 are districts in Basra city. 4 and 6 are small rivers in Basra.

Translated by the poet

Taleb Abdulaziz

Born in Basra, 1952.
Published books:
History of Distress, Baghdad. 1994.
What Can Not Be Unmasked by the Lantern, Damascus.

History of Distress

Those who are aged in love, saints of the date palm,
the young old men,
those who have low foreheads,
those whose backs were bent by the mornings
and their waists were ploughed by the robes,
descendants of deep rivers and pure lineage,
sellers of honey for all time,
players of tambourines, carriers of torches,
and leaders of the caravan —

The aged singers, the players of sad reed pipes,
the ones who come from all directions,
"Suweiq,"[1] who have been fed up for ages
whose smiles never left the faces of their masters,
the makers of glories for others,
drew boats early to the coast
and stayed awake long nights of going and coming
on arcades which were exhausted by water —

Those who filled the warehouses with dates and oil
hung the doors, who went by ships
shadowed by the gray clouds of God.
From the beginning until the end of the sea
one ringing of oars sounded
as a hidden weeping plowed their bodies.
Those whose names were written on steamers, pistons,
oars and the high masts —

Those for whom time engraved drawings
on wet panels that waves drilled
into days and nights,
those for whom the plains witnessed,
and giant ships screamed into their hearts.
They covered their ages with cellophane
and wandered about cities and countries.
Time ate their shoulders
when its flag was their shirts —

The sea addicts, those whom poles
dug holes into their ribs,
their legs jumped like stabbed rabbits
when they walked.
Their faces are like the mediastinums of ships,
sharp and acute,
their sails are their death.
They are breeding sharks at the backs of their boats
and the decks cats are black like teapots.
They hate the land
and in the sea there is too much.
Beneath their green belts are daggers with silver handles.
Those who fed the sea their dear ones
and whales ate their torsos and their potency,
those whose houses have no sofas
and their beds are made of palm branches —

Their rejoicing is deferred always,
they are fools wrapped by robes of hemp
alongside the boats and the cattle.
They never eat their relatives' meat.
If their cows are saved, they are saved from hunger.
They slaughter their best animals for their guests.
The earth is their dining table
and their dishes are made of precious metal.

There is no wine in their houses
and they hide keys and money in salt vessels.
On their walls are anchored ships, eternal pirate
bounty of ivory and sandal
from sunken ships of ancient times.

Since clouds were gray
their bodies have been running in open air.
From their roofs hang stuffed foxes and hedgehogs.
Their doors face the sea and the wind is their shoes.
The smell of water is in their clothes
wrinkled and made ready by waves.
Their eyebrows are thick. They are dim by day
and their necks are large.
Lanterns hung on their roofs leak sorrows and oil
and from the wide jetty, turtles ascend.
They take your boat as they take your hand
and they fasten it to their dearest tree.
On benches, behind which pomegranate blossoms
call out, they stuff your pipe with a special tobacco
prepared for guests.
No matter how sad you are, this antidote will please
you late at night.
Their houses are close to each other
and on the stone walls is written a deep rooted wisdom,
"Stay together because the wolf
eats the single sheep"

Only one way for thieves,
the gunmen are above faithfulness,
their lanterns never go out.
Their tombs are close together and on the banks
of the rivers, tides immerse them everyday.
In the remote tributaries they propagate and grow up.
Mornings take them to different places
and moons with pigs make them return.
Barefooted only from the light of the utmost soul,
on their backs are extinguished suns.

They feel indifferent about the ages
and their days are a bit longer than their trousers.
They are the ones — fond of love,
fond of death,
the wind has eaten their flags.

[1]*Suweiq*: A kind of cheap and not good date.

Translated by: Soheil Najm

Yahya Sahib
Born in Samawah, 1954.
Published book:
A Gazelle From Green Paper, Baghdad 1974.

Clocks

Like summer flowers the clocks turn pale
and fall
in the wood of the café.
A lady crosses.
Her step is like a white dove of love
and when she is absent
the doves remain white
drilling in the dryness of the flowers.
The clocks melt
on the rocks,
a crazy Dali
sleeps with a woman in my paintings.
And I am
        alone,
like a nail
making summer exaltation sick.
On the wood of the café,
I run away from my depths,
I hire the black sea rooms
                (in a swimsuit).
This sea is dissolute.
O, who can cover the nudity of the sea?
Smoke ascends like big horses
in the café.
The brown tea is thick
enough to fasten our lips.
Another woman will enter my paintings,
black-eyed.
      So I pour my insomnia in her eyes
        and stay alone
          like a frightened horse...
If my torture was in you, I would kill you and rest.

On the other hand,
this familiar coffin is coming like
                    my fingers,
charged with tubercular birds,
and the sticks of loneliness,
over my mouth.
Pass like the water and go,
do not turn around.
I'll stay alone,
            in the café,
stripping the flowers off the clocks and tossing them.
The beggar wind comes,
                    takes them,
                    and runs away.

Translated by: Soheil Najm

Zahir al-Jizani

Born in Baghdad, 1948.
Published books:
Come; Let's Go to the Wild, Baghdad 1977,
To Explain the Misunderstanding of the Intention, Baghdad 1981,
Break Down Carriage of the Invaders, 1981,
The Father in His Personal Evening, 1989.

You, Alone, Collect Our Fractures

For Jafar Abu Attemmen[1]

No escape from talking,
yet talking about pain makes it trivial,
talking about crisis stultifies it,
no escape from talking about how Iraq
is melting like a wall of mud in water —
the river of blood and the river of gold are running
between the hands of an executioner
born from an egg — and here they are,
the rest by chance of Anatolian ancestry
and Qureishi[2] spirit
in a boat of Arabism sailing out of a nationalistic system
into a base of hatred that
neither the holy books
nor common history, nor common language,
nor the commonplace can extinguish.

The river of blood and the river of gold
are holding up a boat of Arabism.
It is neither Anatolian nor Arabic,
but a mixture the holy books couldn't stop,
which is why we want to be protected by your
wide cloak, we want you to pull us from the mud,
we who search for our blood in the mouths of the quarries.
The river of blood and the river of gold are running together
between the executioner's hands who was born from an egg.

Time ended too soon when Iraq
was melting like a muddy wall in water,
when I was playing dice blindfolded.
The poem wants to speak of history,
the poem wants to leave the habit of lyricism,
the poem wants to have the power of the Pharaoh,
the poem wants to be history,
and history is a big spy, no groups of killers
can run away from its tattling.

The river of blood and the river of gold are running together
between the executioner hands who was born from an egg.
The yellow around the red is your crown.
In the market they speak of the symbolic exchange
between gold and blood in Iraq so you
come here every morning, down your stairs
to an alley full of the air of old stoves,
full of sellers' gossip and spice dealers' tales.
As if you came down on a carpet,
you are the son of the lamp lightening the street,
you are the son of the wooden window and the big parquet gate,
you are the son of the sky that is sleeping in coffee bags,
you are the last wise man with right words in his mouth,
food and fire in his hands.

The river of blood and the river of gold are running together
between the hands of the executioner who was
born from an egg,
to become a symbolic exchange between domes
and Bedouin raids, the world
in their glassy eyes shines like a farm,
but the world in your black eyes reflects hands
interlaced around one God with different Sharias[3].
In spite of evidence the river split by itself,
you were collecting its shreds
from Bedouin hands. In your wide cloak
you were connecting its fractures.

The river of blood and the river of gold are running together
between the executioner's hands who was
born from an egg —
the symbolic exchange among
massacred peoples. Yet things remained as they were.
Gold and blood attached to each other feeding
Osmotic hatred, the high yellow domes that incite Bedouins
to destroy them, the image of the river that is split on itself,
the horrible change from the worship of Allah
to the worship of power, all this
pale and healthy in Iraq that is melting
like a wall of mud in water.

The river of blood and the river of gold are running together
between the executioner's hands who was
born from an egg —
is Iraq a country or a passage?
"A country when it is for its citizens," you said,
"It is a passage when it is for others, "Salahudin al-Sabbagh[4] said.

Is Iraq a country or a passage?
How great the losses for your followers! Your followers
paid a big cost, as did your opponents.
The rulers are afraid and the Cuban doctors
are ready inside the palace with sharp tools
to change the president's face, the president as he slipped
away among citizens and slept in forlorn houses.
Wars, wars, massacres, massacres, money,
millions of dollars were packed with the garbage.

In the sixties I saw a detective riding a bike
wearing light shoes, his pistol on his hip.
He was sitting in the café, playing dominos, had friends.
All the people knew him, yet there was safety.
In the seventies and the eighties I saw a detective
with golden rings on his fingers driving a super car,
putting on a neat suit. His pockets were filled with golden watches
and bracelets for hunting Iraqi women.

He wanted to kill any man, rape any woman,
didn't know the streets of the city,
didn't know the streetlights, the wooden windows,
the big gates, the coffee packets or the pastry that was mixed
with oil and soaked in tea.
He read neither newspapers nor books.
He was a security man with no education,
brought by military vans
from outlying villages.
Security had faded in Iraq; there was no safety in people's hearts.
Too many bribes paid to the four directions.
Your opponents were also complaining of worn nerves
and the need to sleep. They were killed.
They were shot in front of their colleagues in closed rooms
or open fields when they failed or lagged in killing or hunting.
Your followers and the followers of your opponents
paid the cost, may I expose the documents?

Iraq is for the Iraqis; this is your wisdom,
yet the Iraqis didn't install a statue of you,
and the youths in Baghdad didn't know who you were
and didn't read about you in their schoolbooks.
The poem wants to narrate history.
In 1991 Iraqi Moslem Arab officers attacked and killed
with heavy weapons and mustard gas
Iraqi Moslems, Arabs —
Iraqi Moslems and Iraqi non-Moslems,
in the south and the north of Iraq.
Does religion unite? Does the place unite?
Why did Arabism fail to cast sectarianism
from its soul? Why?
The teacher of the village who lived at the Balkan borders
during 1916 wanted to confirm the same pain.
"Ottoman is the bond of the kingdoms," he said.
as if the Inkishari[5] were absent.
The stories about exemplary punishment are refuting
all his examples.

Should I narrate stories of Mohammed Tahir al-Umari
in 1914?

The teacher of the village who fled from Balkan borders
returned again to Baghdad in 1922 to say
that language is the bond of nationality.
Military brigades formed immediately, and immediately
the rivers of blood and the rivers of gold ran in Iraq
that is melting as a wall of mud in water.

Corruption was stronger than everyone.
Ideology like the snake tongue killed every thing
and language became no longer communication
or a common cognition, it became an ideology
and identity no longer became an identity alone
in Seebeweih's[6] book or al-Tabari's[7] book,
identity became larger than language. May I expose
the documents? Show how the common history
was thrown in the garbage? Is the party stronger than
language and history? What was it, that authority
with the right to own and cancel us?

History is a great spy. Death squads will never
flee from its tattling. There is something else
we have to explain in detail, something else
more important than religion, and that is our relationship
to the other. Is the other my partner, or an enemy to defeat?
At this juncture executioners are born. This black
and complicated point is like the egg of a horrible creature
from which executioners are always born.
Those who dissect the truth say it is the public
agony of the other, and those who dissect power
say the same thing. Somebody said that power
is the cause of the agony of the other.
Neither truth nor Satan can be sure of their place.
Language has a poisoned tongue too,
it can kill us as we survive if it wants to.
The adjective fabricates what it describes.

The adjective that is the tongue of language and its image
of the world is a hundred percent fake.
Time passed too when Iraq was melting
like a wall of mud in water. Zarathustra's promise
could not stand against the immediacy of evil.

No, I will not chant spells and I will not be
a magician since the history of chanting weakened our ability
to hunt Satan and man lies dying in long agony alongside
the Holy Books – explanations moving rapidly
from one place to another – continuous displacements
based on surnames, nicknames and morals,
continuous displacements based on criteria and roles
that are historically unbelievable, written from
the solitary point of view of the executioner.
Adjectives change every hour – the faithful and the traitor
change places continuously and the adjective
fabricates new reality every hour – death squads
want to cheat God, to write all his names in their blood.

And those who are slaughtered have the same documents
and the same explanations. I'll not be a magician. Magic
is a random point in the soul, and I'll not be a lyricist,
the history of lyricism is misleading the truth,
and man is dying in long agony
alongside his history, where motives don't change.
In order to survive one must occupy the other –
the culture of Satan is also the culture of the historical hero.
And weak is the artist's soul, cruel is the power
of the party. The image of a jet in Albab Asharqi,[8]
the image of a wooden seat in a park
are more important than the image of a soldier
as he destroys an iron gate in the Alhurria
monument of Jewad Salim. [9]
What soldier can destroy the Iron Gate?
So soon your time had ended. So strong
was your barrier. Neither party nor sect

nor nationality, nor religion prevailed.
Iraqis had already tried all the shelters of death, from
the backstreets, to a new country, to hearts which will merge.
The youth of Baghdad will see your statue.
This poem is for you — you alone
collect our fractures that are thrown into the streets.

[1] Jaffar Abu Attemen: Iraqi nationalist politician who was able to gather the Sunnis and the Shiites against the English occupation of Iraq from 1920 till he died in 1945.
[2] Qureish: An Arabian tribe, to which the prophet Mohammed belonged.
[3] Islamic law.
[4] Salahudin al-Sabbagh: One the four officers who were executed in 1941 after the fall of their military movement against the English occupation.
[5] Inkishari: A Turkish soldier.
[6] Seebeweih: An old Arabic linguist.
[7] Al-Tabari: An old Arabic historian.
[8] Albab al-Sharqi: The east gate of Baghdad.
[9] Jewad Salim (1921-1961) Iraqi well known sculptor who sculpted the famous momument of freedom (Alhurria).

Translated by: Soheil Najm

Zaeem al-Nassar
Born in Nasiria, al-Qala'a 1957.

On the Way
Until the Hidden Statue Falls Down

On the way
to the fog tavern,
to the tavern of drunkenness,
to a young girl in al-Qala'a
who says, "Something has disappeared."

There is no way,
there is no way for you,
there is no way for a bright guitar.
Nothing but spiders sucking
the light of speech.
There is no way to the coast
that is awaiting your star.
There is no way for the hope
floating in your blood.
You'll remain stymied
until the hidden statue falls down.

There is no way to your way.
The eyes of the fake men
are watching you.
Do you know that?
Yet the wind is an eye for you.

So
you will build a village
in a cup of craziness
and see the strings of your guitar
vibrate on a moon
coming up from the depths of the Euphrates.
You have winds coming up
to erase the fog
from the mirror

wearing the mask of hope
so the road leads you on
to its young girl,
to its tavern,
to its awakening
until you, the guitar and the wind sink deep
into Al-Qala'a's river
for ever.

Translated by: Soheil Najm

Ziara Mehdi
Born in Baghdad, 1955.
Published book:
Thresholds, Baghdad, 1978.

A Tree on the Horizon

Are these your braids
or the nests of legends..?

○

Come in the spaces of the poem
O, tree
come in…
you will see how the language breaks
and returns to its root ... which is your root.

○

Come into my creative context
then go out ... like a call in the sky.

○

Go out…
so that I can see the crowds
running naked towards you
running ...running
because they are ...
all Adam
and only you are Eve.

◯

I saw al-Nawasi[1].
O tree,
throwing his cup
and coming down from the hillock of this time.
I saw him…
taking off his jubbah
throwing his turban to the horizon.
I saw him … kneeling
but suddenly he stood up
and ran to the tree.
I saw him
dangling between two boughs crying!!

◯

O, al-Nawasi
you have no hope to ascend…
you'll stay suspended…like this
since you didn't write one poem
for a country eaten by wars.

◯

I withdraw…
O tree,
I withdraw … till the scene widens
and the phrase shrinks.
I withdraw…
I withdraw…
I know that Tigris is behind me.
I withdraw…
I withdraw…

All of them are Adam
O tree
and you are the only Eve.
I withdraw…
I withdraw…
I with…
I…

O, for Adam whose stature interlaced
among your branches
and disappeared
in the tensions of the sap.

¹ al-Nawasi is a renown Abbasid poet who was well known for his poems about wine.

Translated by: Soheil Najm

Why Do I Wave?

Every time…
I listen to my reflection in the water
I am multiplied
as if a million formal mirrors
were standing to humiliate me…!
Who am I
to be loosened…like this,
like sails…interring in the winds' breaking..?
Sails… every time
nature exhausts them…they hide in my orbit.

O

I am
the center of eternity
and the marble of its history.
I am the Sumerian dropped by a severe universe,
dropped, in the seas of time
and told —
"Do not … do not be wet with water."

O

The guides … I follow them.
caring only for the sailor
whose boats disappoint him,
coasts gone to mire …
The guides justified our sad swamps,
his swamps … that didn't stop
from rudeness … to the land.
That sailor,
every time
he sees the south birds
listening

to their image in the waters,
he provokes them,
so the birds fly
past even their skies.

O

O, for the cranes that leave him
alone …
the flock of disaster
that gathers in miserable and blind space.

O

Why do I rise in waves
in response to the earth?
Its feasts are collapsing …
the earth … rotating
like the rotation of the guillotine,
rotating as if its autumn were the first of the resurrection,
a wide resurrection,
as if it were the rising of firewood,
a resurrection …
flaming up with the wind,
rushing to
the flame's uprising.

O

How much dignity in ash
can humiliate the forest..?

O

Glory to the sparrows…and the splendor of flying.
That's what the trees said.
Glory to the poets.
They have space, we circle shyly.
They have conditions.
We moisten them with the saliva of the farms.
Who are we
but the silver of the water…setting up from the flexibility of the reed,
the agony of cane…allowing the south to remain nimble.

Translated by: Soheil Najm

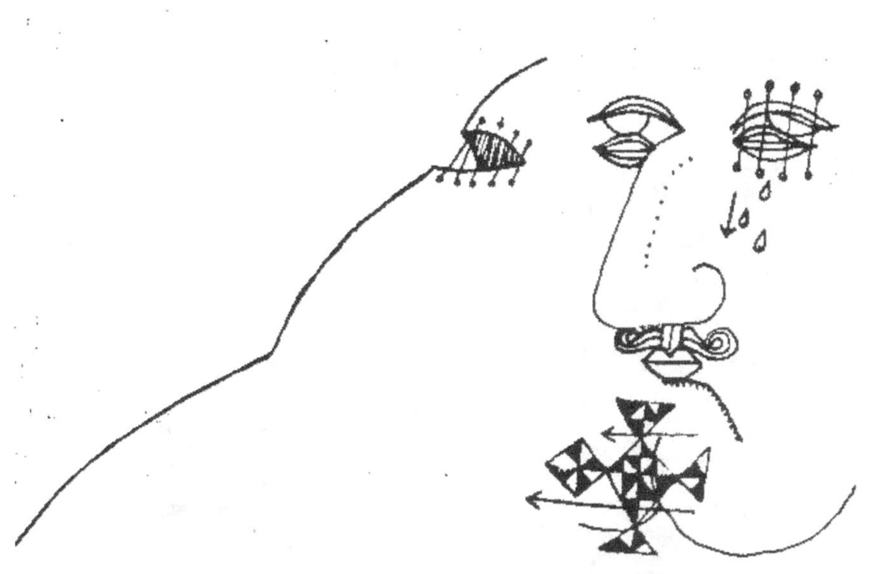

Art by Khalid Khudayer.

Iraqi poets reading in Baghdad along the Tigris River in a poetry series hosted by the House of Iraqi Poetry and at a church that was, the week before, attacked by terrrorists.

Art by Sadiq Assaieg

About the Translators

Soheil Najm was born in Baghdad in 1956. An internationally known poet and translator, he is author of *Breaking the Phrase* (Beirut, 1994), *I Am Your Carpenter, Oh Light* (Damascus, 2002) and *No Paradise Outside the Window* (Baghdad, 2008), and translator into Arabic of *The Gospel According to Jesus Christ* by Jose Saramago and *The Serpent and the Lily* by Nikos Kazantzakis. Soheil was the editor of *Gilgamesh*, Iraq's cultural magazine in English and is now the editor of the journal, *Foreign Culture*, in Arabic.

Sadek Mohammed was born in 1964. He holds a Ph.D. in English Literature from Pune University in India. Currently he is Associate Professor of English at Al-Mustansiriyah University in Baghdad, and serves as an editor of *Gilgamesh*, Iraq's cultural magazine in English.